Mastering OpenCV Android Application Programming

Master the art of implementing computer vision algorithms on Android platforms to build robust and efficient applications

Salil Kapur

Nisarg Thakkar

[PACKT] open source*

PUBLISHING

community experience distilled

BIRMINGHAM - MUMBAI

Mastering OpenCV Android Application Programming

First published: July 2015

Production reference: 1230715

Published by Packt Publishing Ltd.
Livery Place
35 Livery Street
Birmingham B3 2PB, UK.

ISBN 978-1-78398-820-4

www.packtpub.com

Credits

Authors

Salil Kapur

Nisarg Thakkar

Reviewers

Radhakrishna Dasari

Noritsuna Imamura

Ashwin Kachhara

André Moreira de Souza

Commissioning Editor

Kartikey Pandey

Acquisition Editors

Harsha Bharwani

Aditya Nair

Content Development Editors

Ruchita Bhansali

Kirti Patil

Technical Editor

Ankur Ghiye

Copy Editor

Rashmi Sawant

Project Coordinator

Nidhi Joshi

Proofreader

Safis Editing

Indexer

Hemangini Bari

Graphics

Sheetal Aute

Production Coordinator

Nitesh Thakur

Cover Work

Nitesh Thakur

About the Authors

Salil Kapur is a software engineer at Microsoft. He earned his bachelor's degree in computer science from Birla Institute of Technology and Science, Pilani.

He has a passion for programming and is always excited to try out new technologies. His interests lie in computer vision, networks, and developing scalable systems. He is an open source enthusiast and has contributed to libraries such as SimpleCV, BinPy, and Krita.

When he is not working, he spends most of his time on Quora and Hacker News. He loves to play basketball and ultimate frisbee. He can be reached at salilkapur93@gmail.com.

Nisarg Thakkar is a software developer and a tech enthusiast in general. He primarily programs in C++ and Java. He has extensive experience in Android app development and computer vision application development using OpenCV. He has also contributed to an OpenCV project and works on its development during his free time. His interests lie in stereo vision, virtual reality, and exploiting the Android platform for noncommercial projects that benefit the people who cannot afford the conventional solutions.

He was also the subcoordinator of the Mobile App Club at his university. He was also the cofounder of two start-ups at his college, which he started with his group of friends. One of these start-ups has developed Android apps for hotels, while the other is currently working on building a better contact manager app for the Android platform.

Nisarg Thakkar is currently studying at BITS Pilani, K. K. Birla Goa campus, where he will be graduating with a degree in engineering (hons.) in computer science in May 2016. He can be reached at nisargtha@gmail.com.

About the Reviewers

Radhakrishna Dasari is a computer science PhD student at the State University of New York in Buffalo. He works at Ubiquitous Multimedia Lab, whose director is Dr. Chang Wen Chen. His research spans computer vision and machine learning with an emphasis on multimedia applications. He intends to pursue a research career in computer vision and loves to teach.

Noritsuna Imamura is a specialist in embedded Linux/Android-based computer vision. He is the main person of SIProp (http://siprop.org/).

His main works are as follows:

- ITRI Smart Glass, which is similar to Google Glass. He worked on this using Android 4.3 and OpenCV 2.4 in June 2014 (https://www.itri.org.tw/chi/Content/techTransfer/tech_tran_cont.aspx?&SiteID=1&MmmID=620622510147005345&Keyword=&MSid=4858).

- Treasure Hunting Robot, a brainwave controlling robot that he developed in February 2012 (http://www.siprop.org/en/2.0/index.php?product%2FTreasureHuntingRobot).

- OpenCV for Android NDK. This has been included since Android 4.0.1 (http://tools.oesf.biz/android-4.0.1_r1.0/search?q=SIProp).

- Auto Chasing Turtle, a human face recognition robot with Kinect, which he developed in February 2011 (http://www.siprop.org/ja/2.0/index.php?product%2FAutoChasingTurtle).

- Feel sketch—an AR Authoring Tool and AR Browser as an Android application, which he developed in December 2009 (http://code.google.com/p/feelsketch/).

He can be reached at noritsuna@siprop.org.

Ashwin Kachhara graduated from IIT Bombay in June 2015 and is currently pursuing his master's at Georgia Tech, Atlanta. Over the past 5 years, he has been developing software for different platforms, including AVR, Android, Microsoft Kinect, and the Oculus Rift. His professional interests span Mixed Reality, Wearable Technologies, graphics, and computer vision. He has previously worked as an intern at the SONY Head Mounted Display (HMD) division in Tokyo and at the National University of Singapore's Interactive and Digital Media Institute (IDMI). He is a virtual reality enthusiast and enjoys rollerblading and karaoke when he is not writing awesome code.

André Moreira de Souza is a PhD candidate in computer science, with an emphasis on computer graphics from the Pontifical Catholic University of Rio de Janeiro (Brazil).

He graduated with a bachelor of computer science degree from Universidade Federal do Maranhão (UFMA) in Brazil. During his undergraduate degree, he was a member of Labmint's research team and worked with medical imaging, specifically, breast cancer detection and diagnosis using image processing.

Currently, he works as a researcher and system analyst at Instituto Tecgraf, one of the major research and development labs in computer graphics in Brazil. He has been working extensively with PHP, HTML, and CSS since 2007; nowadays, he develops projects in C++11/C++14, along with SQLite, Qt, Boost, and OpenGL. More information about him can be acquired by visiting his personal website at www.andredsm.com.

www.PacktPub.com

Support files, eBooks, discount offers, and more

For support files and downloads related to your book, please visit www.PacktPub.com.

Did you know that Packt offers eBook versions of every book published, with PDF and ePub files available? You can upgrade to the eBook version at www.PacktPub.com and as a print book customer, you are entitled to a discount on the eBook copy. Get in touch with us at service@packtpub.com for more details.

At www.PacktPub.com, you can also read a collection of free technical articles, sign up for a range of free newsletters and receive exclusive discounts and offers on Packt books and eBooks.

https://www2.packtpub.com/books/subscription/packtlib

Do you need instant solutions to your IT questions? PacktLib is Packt's online digital book library. Here, you can search, access, and read Packt's entire library of books.

Why subscribe?

- Fully searchable across every book published by Packt
- Copy and paste, print, and bookmark content
- On demand and accessible via a web browser

Free access for Packt account holders

If you have an account with Packt at www.PacktPub.com, you can use this to access PacktLib today and view 9 entirely free books. Simply use your login credentials for immediate access.

Table of Contents

Preface   **v**

Chapter 1: Applying Effects to Images   **1**

  Getting started   2
  Setting up OpenCV   2
  Storing images in OpenCV   4
  Linear filters in OpenCV   5
    The mean blur method   6
    The Gaussian blur method   12
    The median blur method   14
    Creating custom kernels   15
    Morphological operations   16
      Dilation   16
      Erosion   18
    Thresholding   19
    Adaptive thresholding   20
  Summary   **21**

Chapter 2: Detecting Basic Features in Images   **23**

  Creating our application   23
  Edge and Corner detection   28
    The difference of Gaussian technique   29
    The Canny Edge detector   32
    The Sobel operator   34
    Harris Corner detection   36

Hough transformations	**38**
Hough lines	38
Hough circles	40
Contours	**42**
Project – detecting a Sudoku puzzle in an image	**44**
Summary	**46**
Chapter 3: Detecting Objects	**47**
What are features?	**47**
Scale Invariant Feature Transform	**48**
Understanding how SIFT works	49
Scale-space extrema detection	49
Keypoint localization	52
Orientation assignment	54
Keypoint descriptor	55
SIFT in OpenCV	57
Matching features and detecting objects	**59**
Brute-force matcher	60
FLANN based matcher	60
Matching the points	60
Detecting objects	64
Speeded Up Robust Features	**65**
SURF detector	65
SURF descriptor	67
SURF in OpenCV	69
Oriented FAST and Rotated BRIEF	**70**
oFAST – FAST keypoint orientation	70
FAST detector	70
Orientation by intensity centroid	71
rBRIEF – Rotation-aware BRIEF	71
Steered BRIEF	72
Variance and correlation	72
ORB in OpenCV	73
Binary Robust Invariant Scalable Keypoints	**74**
Scale-space keypoint detection	74
Keypoint description	76
Sampling pattern and rotation estimation	76
Building the descriptor	77
BRISK In OpenCV	78
Fast Retina Keypoint	**79**
A retinal sampling pattern	79
A coarse-to-fine descriptor	80
Saccadic search	80

Orientation	81
FREAK in OpenCV	81
Summary	**82**
Chapter 4: Drilling Deeper into Object Detection – Using Cascade Classifiers	**83**
An introduction to cascade classifiers	**84**
Haar cascades	84
LBP cascades	85
Face detection using the cascade classifier	**86**
HOG descriptors	**93**
Project – Happy Camera	**96**
Summary	**97**
Chapter 5: Tracking Objects in Videos	**99**
Optical flow	**99**
The Horn and Schunck method	101
The Lucas and Kanade method	101
Checking out the optical flow on Android	105
Image pyramids	**111**
Gaussian pyramids	112
Laplacian pyramids	114
Gaussian and Laplacian pyramids in OpenCV	114
Basic 2D transformations	**120**
Global motion estimation	**122**
The Kanade-Lucas-Tomasi tracker	**125**
Checking out the KLT tracker on OpenCV	125
Summary	**127**
Chapter 6: Working with Image Alignment and Stitching	**129**
Image stitching	**129**
Feature detection and matching	130
Image matching	132
Homography estimation using RANSAC	132
Verification of image matches using a probabilistic model	132
Bundle adjustment	134
Automatic panoramic straightening	134
Gain compensation	135
Multi-band blending	136
Image stitching using OpenCV	137
Setting up Android NDK	138
The layout and Java code	139
The C++ code	143
Summary	**147**

Chapter 7: Bringing Your Apps to Life with OpenCV Machine Learning — **149**

Optical Character Recognition — **150**
  OCR using k-nearest neighbors — 150
    Making a camera application — 151
    Handling the training data — 153
    Recognizing digits — 158
  OCR using Support Vector Machines — 160
Solving a Sudoku puzzle — **162**
  Recognizing digits in the puzzle — 162
Summary — **164**

Chapter 8: Troubleshooting and Best Practices — **165**

Troubleshooting errors — **165**
  Permission errors — 165
    Some common permissions — 167
  Debugging code using Logcat — 168
Best practices — **169**
  Handling images in Android — 170
    Loading images — 170
    Processing images — 171
  Handling data between multiple activities — 172
    Transferring data via Intent — 173
    Using static fields — 173
    Using a database or a file — 174
Summary — **174**

Chapter 9: Developing a Document Scanning App — **175**

Let's begin — **176**
The algorithm — **177**
Implementing on Android — **179**
Summary — **190**

Index — **191**

Preface

This book will help you get started with OpenCV on the Android platform in no time. It explains the various computer vision algorithms conceptually, as well as their implementation on the Android platform. This book is an invaluable resource if you are looking forward to implementing computer vision modules on new or existing Android apps.

What this book covers

Chapter 1, Applying Effects to Images, includes some of the basic preprocessing algorithms used in various computer vision applications. This chapter also explains how you can integrate OpenCV to your existing projects.

Chapter 2, Detecting Basic Features in Images, covers the detection of primary features such as edges, corners, lines, and circles in images.

Chapter 3, Detecting Objects, dives deep into feature detection, using more advanced algorithms to detect and describe features in order to uniquely match them to features in other objects.

Chapter 4, Drilling Deeper into Object Detection – Using Cascade Classifiers, explains the detection of general objects, such as faces/eyes in images and videos.

Chapter 5, Tracking Objects in Videos, covers the concepts of optical flow as a motion detector and implements the Lucas-Kanade-Tomasi tracker to track objects in a video.

Chapter 6, Working with Image Alignment and Stitching, covers the basic concepts of image alignment and image stitching to create a panoramic scene image.

Chapter 7, Bringing Your Apps to Life with OpenCV Machine Learning, explains how machine learning can be used in computer vision applications. In this chapter, we take a look at some common machine learning algorithms and their implementation in Android.

Chapter 8, Troubleshooting and Best Practices, covers some of the common errors and issues that developers face while building their applications. It also unfolds some good practices that can make the application more efficient.

Chapter 9, Developing a Document Scanning App, uses various algorithms that have been explained across various chapters to build a complete system to scan documents, regardless of what angle you click the image at.

What you need for this book

For this book, you need a system with at least 1 GB RAM. Windows, OS X, and Linux are the currently supported operating systems for Android development.

Who this book is for

If you are a Java and Android developer and looking to enhance your skills by learning the latest features of OpenCV Android application programming, then this book is for you.

Conventions

In this book, you will find a number of text styles that distinguish between different kinds of information. Here are some examples of these styles and an explanation of their meaning.

Code words in text, database table names, folder names, filenames, file extensions, pathnames, dummy URLs, user input, and Twitter handles are shown as follows: "Create a file named `Application.mk` and copy the following lines of code to it."

A block of code is set as follows:

```
<uses-permission android:name="android.permission.CAMERA"/>
    <uses-feature android:name="android.hardware.camera"
      android:required="false"/>
```

```
<uses-feature android:name="android.hardware.camera.autofocus"
  android:required="false"/>
<uses-feature android:name="android.hardware.camera.front"
  android:required="false"/>
<uses-feature android:name="android.hardware.camera.
  front.autofocus" android:required="false"/>
```

New terms and **important words** are shown in bold.

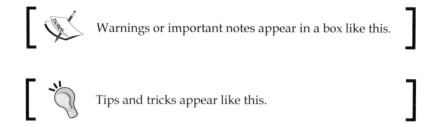

Warnings or important notes appear in a box like this.

Tips and tricks appear like this.

Reader feedback

Feedback from our readers is always welcome. Let us know what you think about this book—what you liked or disliked. Reader feedback is important for us as it helps us develop titles that you will really get the most out of.

To send us general feedback, simply e-mail feedback@packtpub.com, and mention the book's title in the subject of your message.

If there is a topic that you have expertise in and you are interested in either writing or contributing to a book, see our author guide at www.packtpub.com/authors.

Customer support

Now that you are the proud owner of a Packt book, we have a number of things to help you to get the most from your purchase.

Downloading the example code

You can download the example code files from your account at http://www.packtpub.com for all the Packt Publishing books you have purchased. If you purchased this book elsewhere, you can visit http://www.packtpub.com/support and register to have the files e-mailed directly to you.

Downloading the color images of this book

We also provide you with a PDF file that has color images of the screenshots/ diagrams used in this book. The color images will help you better understand the changes in the output. You can download this file from: `https://www.packtpub.com/sites/default/files/downloads/8204OS_ImageBundle.pdf`.

Errata

Although we have taken every care to ensure the accuracy of our content, mistakes do happen. If you find a mistake in one of our books—maybe a mistake in the text or the code—we would be grateful if you could report this to us. By doing so, you can save other readers from frustration and help us improve subsequent versions of this book. If you find any errata, please report them by visiting `http://www.packtpub.com/submit-errata`, selecting your book, clicking on the **Errata Submission Form** link, and entering the details of your errata. Once your errata are verified, your submission will be accepted and the errata will be uploaded to our website or added to any list of existing errata under the Errata section of that title.

To view the previously submitted errata, go to `https://www.packtpub.com/books/content/support` and enter the name of the book in the search field. The required information will appear under the **Errata** section.

Piracy

Piracy of copyrighted material on the Internet is an ongoing problem across all media. At Packt, we take the protection of our copyright and licenses very seriously. If you come across any illegal copies of our works in any form on the Internet, please provide us with the location address or website name immediately so that we can pursue a remedy.

Please contact us at `copyright@packtpub.com` with a link to the suspected pirated material.

We appreciate your help in protecting our authors and our ability to bring you valuable content.

Questions

If you have a problem with any aspect of this book, you can contact us at `questions@packtpub.com`, and we will do our best to address the problem.

1
Applying Effects to Images

Generally, an image contains more information than required for any particular task. For this reason, we need to preprocess the images so that they contain only as much information as required for the application, thereby reducing the computing time needed.

In this chapter, we will learn about the different preprocessing operations, which are as follows:

- Blurring
- De-noising
- Sharpening
- Erosion and dilation
- Thresholding and adaptive thresholding

At the end of this chapter, we will see how you can integrate OpenCV into your existing Android applications.

Before we take a look at the various feature detection algorithms and their implementations, let's first build a basic Android application to which we will keep adding feature detection algorithms, as we go through this chapter.

Getting started

When we see an image, we perceive it as colors and objects. However, a computer vision system sees it as a matrix of numbers (see the following image). These numbers are interpreted differently, depending on the color model used. The computer cannot directly detect patterns or objects in the image. The aim of computer vision systems is to interpret this matrix of numbers as an object of a particular type.

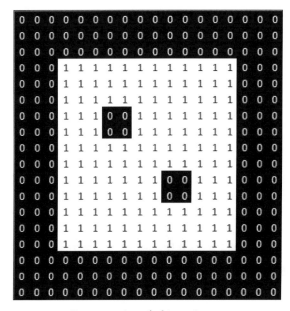

Representation of a binary image

Setting up OpenCV

OpenCV is the short form of Open Source Computer Vision library. It is the most widely used computer vision library. It is a collection of commonly used functions that perform operations related to computer vision. OpenCV has been natively written in C/C++, but has wrappers for Python, Java, and any JVM language, which is designed to create the Java byte code, such as Scala and Clojure. Since most of the Android app development is done in C++/Java, OpenCV has also been ported as an SDK that developers can use to implement it in their apps and make them vision enabled.

We will now take a look at how to get started with setting up OpenCV for the Android platform, and start our journey. We will use Android Studio as our IDE of choice, but any other IDE should work just as well with slight modifications. Follow these steps in order to get started:

1. Download Android Studio from `https://developer.android.com/sdk/` and OpenCV4Android SDK from `http://sourceforge.net/projects/opencvlibrary/files/opencv-android/`.

2. Extract the two files to a known location.

3. Create a normal Android Project and name it `FirstOpenCVApp`. Navigate to **File | Import**.

4. Select the `OpenCV_SDK_location/sdk/java/` directory.

5. Navigate to **Build | Rebuild Project**.

6. Navigate to **File | Project Structure**.

7. Add the OpenCV module to your app by selecting the **app** module in the left column. Click on the green in the dependencies tab, and finally, select the OpenCV module.

8. You are now ready to use OpenCV in your Android project. It should look like this:

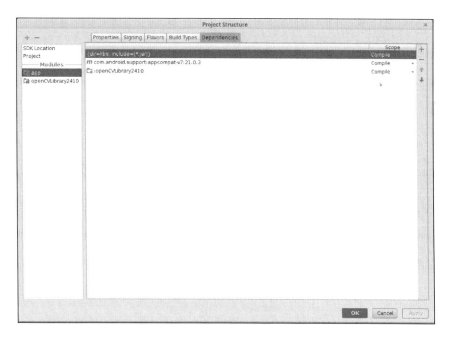

Storing images in OpenCV

OpenCV stores images as a custom object called **Mat**. This object stores the information such as rows, columns, data, and so on that can be used to uniquely identify and recreate the image when required. Different images contain different amounts of data. For example, a colored image contains more data than a grayscale version of the same image. This is because a colored image is a 3-channel image when using the RGB model, and a grayscale image is a 1-channel image. The following figures show how 1-channel and multichannel (here, RGB) images are stored (these images are taken from docs.opencv.org).

A 1-channel representation of an image is shown as follows:

	Column 0	Column 1	Column ...	Column m
Row 0	0,0	0,1	...	0, m
Row 1	1,0	1,1	...	1, m
Row ...	...,0	...,1	...	..., m
Row n	n,0	n,1	n,...	n, m

A grayscale (1-channel) image representation:

A more elaborate form of an image is the RGB representation, which is shown as follows:

	Column 0			Column 1			Column ...			Column m		
Row 0	0,0	0,0		0,1	0,1	0,1		...		0, m	0, m	0, m
Row 1	1,0	1,0		1,1	1,1	1,1		...		1, m	1, m	1, m
Row ...| 0	...,0			1	...,1			...|	m	..., m		m
Row n	n,0	n,0		n,1	n,1	n,...		n,...		n, m	n, m	n, m

A RGB (3-channel) image representation

In the grayscale image, the numbers represent the intensity of that particular color. They are represented on a scale of 0-255 when using integer representations, with 0 being pure black and 255 being pure white. If we use a floating point representation, the pixels are represented on a scale of 0-1, with 0 being pure black and 1 being pure white. In an RGB image in OpenCV, the first channel corresponds to blue color, second channel corresponds to green color, and the third channel corresponds to red color. Thus, each channel represents the intensity of any particular color. As we know that red, green, and blue are primary colors, they can be combined in different proportions to generate any color visible to the human eye. The following figure shows the different colors and their respective RGB equivalents in an integer format:

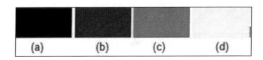

(a)   R=0   G=0   B=0

(b)   R=10   G=20   B=100

(d)   R=255   G=255   B=0

(c)   R=255   G=0   B=0

Now that we have seen how an image is represented in computing terms, we will see how we can modify the pixel values so that they need less computation time when using them for the actual task at hand.

Linear filters in OpenCV

We all like sharp images. Who doesn't, right? However, there is a trade-off that needs to be made. More information means that the image will require more computation time to complete the same task as compared to an image which has less information. So, to solve this problem, we apply blurring operations.

Many of the linear filtering algorithms make use of an array of numbers called a kernel. A kernel can be thought of as a sliding window that passes over each pixel and calculates the output value for that pixel. This can be understood more clearly by taking a look at the following figure (this image of linear filtering/convolution is taken from http://test.virtual-labs.ac.in/labs/cse19/neigh/convolution. jpg):

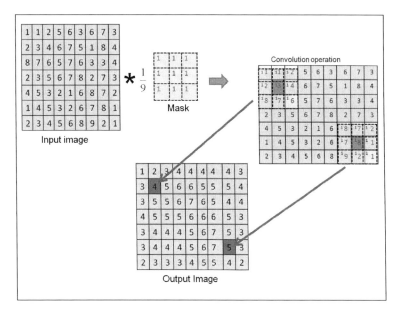

In the preceding figure, a 3 x 3 kernel is used on a 10 x 10 image.

One of the most general operations used for linear filtering is convolution. The values in a kernel are coefficients for multiplication of the corresponding pixels. The final result is stored in the anchor point, generally, the center of the kernel:

$$dst(x,y) = \frac{\sum \left[src(x+i,y+j)*kernel(A+i,B+j) \right]}{\sum \left[kernel(A+i,B+j) \right]}$$

1) A,B is location of anchor pixel

2) Range of i,j depends on anchor pixel

 Linear filtering operations are generally not in-place operations, as for each pixel we use the values present in the original image, and not the modified values.

One of the most common uses of linear filtering is to remove the noise. Noise is the random variation in brightness or color information in images. We use blurring operations to reduce the noise in images.

The mean blur method

A mean filter is the simplest form of blurring. It calculates the mean of all the pixels that the given kernel superimposes. The kernel that is used for this kind of operation is a simple Mat that has all its values as 1, that is, each neighboring pixel is given the same weightage.

For this chapter, we will pick an image from the gallery and apply the respective image transformations. For this, we will add basic code. We are assuming that OpenCV4Android SDK has been set up and is running.

We can use the first OpenCV app that we created at the start of the chapter for the purpose of this chapter. At the time of creating the project, the default names will be as shown in the following screenshot:

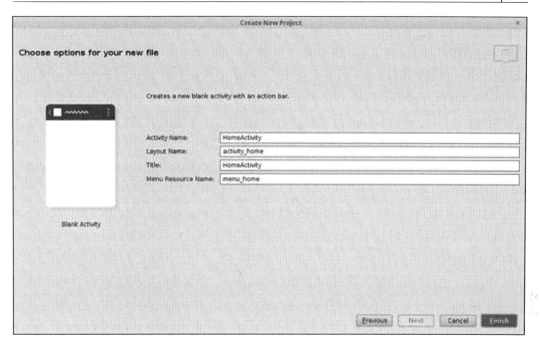

Add a new activity by right-clicking on the Java folder and navigate to **New |
Activity**. Then, select **Blank Activity**. Name the activity `MainActivity.java` and
the XML file `activity_main.xml`. Go to `res/menu/menu_main.xml`. Add an
item as follows:

```
<item android:id="@+id/action_load_image"
      android:title="@string/action_load_image"
      android:orderInCategory="1"
      android:showAsAction="ifRoom" />
```

Since `MainActivity` is the activity that we will be using to perform our OpenCV
specific tasks, we need to instantiate OpenCV. Add this as a global member of
`MainActivity.java`:

```
private BaseLoaderCallback mOpenCVCallBack = new
BaseLoaderCallback(this) {
      @Override
      public void onManagerConnected(int status) {
          switch (status) {
              case LoaderCallbackInterface.SUCCESS:
                  //DO YOUR WORK/STUFF HERE
                  break;
              default:
                  super.onManagerConnected(status);
                  break;
          }
```

```
            }
        };
    @Override
        protected void onResume() {
            super.onResume();
            OpenCVLoader.initAsync(OpenCVLoader.OPENCV_VERSION_2_4_10,
              this,
                    mOpenCVCallBack);
        }
```

This is a callback, which checks whether the OpenCV manager is installed. We need the OpenCV manager app to be installed on the device because it has all of the OpenCV functions defined. If we do not wish to use the OpenCV manager, we can have the functions present natively, but the APK size then increases significantly. If the OpenCV manager is not present, the app redirects the user to the Play Store to download it. The function call in onResume loads OpenCV for use.

Next we will add a button to activity_home.xml:

```
<Button
            android:id="@+id/bMean"
            android:layout_height="wrap_content"
            android:layout_width="wrap_content"
            android:text="Mean Blur" />
```

Then, in HomeActivity.java, we will instantiate this button, and set an onClickListener to this button:

```
Button bMean = (Button)findViewById(R.id.bMean);
bMean.setOnClickListener(new View.OnClickListener() {
            @Override
            public void onClick(View v) {
                Intent i = new Intent(getApplicationContext(),
                  MainActivity.class);
                i.putExtra("ACTION_MODE", MEAN_BLUR);
                startActivity(i);
            }
        });
```

Downloading the example code

You can download the example code files from your account at http://www.packtpub.com for all the Packt Publishing books you have purchased. If you purchased this book elsewhere, you can visit http://www.packtpub.com/support and register to have the files e-mailed directly to you.

In the preceding code, MEAN_BLUR is a constant with value 1 that specifies the type of operation that we want to perform.

Here we have added extra to the activity bundle. This is to differentiate which operation we will be performing.

Open activity_main.xml. Replace everything with this code snippet. This snippet adds two ImageView items: one for the original image and one for the processed image:

```xml
<?xml version="1.0" encoding="utf-8"?>
<LinearLayout xmlns:android="http://schemas.android.com/apk/res/
android"
    android:orientation="vertical"
    android:layout_width="match_parent"
    android:layout_height="match_parent">

    <ImageView
        android:layout_width="match_parent"
        android:layout_height="match_parent"
        android:layout_weight="0.5"
        android:id="@+id/ivImage" />

    <ImageView
        android:layout_width="match_parent"
        android:layout_height="match_parent"
        android:layout_weight="0.5"
        android:id="@+id/ivImageProcessed" />

</LinearLayout>
```

We need to programmatically link these ImageView items to the ImageView items in Java in our MainActivity.java:

```java
    private final int SELECT_PHOTO = 1;
    private ImageView ivImage, ivImageProcessed;
    Mat src;
    static int ACTION_MODE = 0;

    @Override
```

```
    protected void onCreate(Bundle savedInstanceState) {
// Android specific code
ivImage = (ImageView)findViewById(R.id.ivImage);
        ivImageProcessed =
          (ImageView)findViewById(R.id.ivImageProcessed);
        Intent intent = getIntent();

        if(intent.hasExtra("ACTION_MODE")){
            ACTION_MODE = intent.getIntExtra("ACTION_MODE", 0);
    }
```

Here, the Mat and ImageViews have been made global to the class so that we can use them in other functions, without passing them as parameters. We will use the ACTION_MODE variable to identify the required operation to be performed.

Now we will add the code to load an image from the gallery. For this, we will use the menu button we created earlier. We will load the menu_main.xml file, when you click on the menu button:

```
@Override
    public boolean onCreateOptionsMenu(Menu menu) {
        getMenuInflater().inflate(R.menu.menu_main, menu);
        return true;
    }
```

Then we will add the listener that will perform the desired action when an action item is selected. We will use Intent.ACTION_PICK to get an image from the gallery:

```
        @Override
        public boolean onOptionsItemSelected(MenuItem item) {
            int id = item.getItemId();
            if (id == R.id.action_load_image) {
                Intent photoPickerIntent = new
                  Intent(Intent.ACTION_PICK);
                photoPickerIntent.setType("image/*");
                startActivityForResult(photoPickerIntent,
                  SELECT_PHOTO);
                return true;
            }
            return super.onOptionsItemSelected(item);
        }
```

As you can see, we have used `startActivityForResult()`. This will send the selected image to `onActivityResult()`. We will use this to get the Bitmap and convert it to an OpenCV Mat. Once the operation is complete, we want to get the image back from the other activity. For this, we make a new function `onActivityResult()` that gets called when the activity has completed its work, and is returned to the calling activity. Add the following code to `onActivityResult()`:

```
switch(requestCode) {
    case SELECT_PHOTO:
        if(resultCode == RESULT_OK){
            try {
                //Code to load image into a Bitmap and
                    convert it to a Mat for processing.
        final Uri imageUri = imageReturnedIntent.getData();
        final InputStream imageStream =
          getContentResolver().openInputStream(imageUri);
        final Bitmap selectedImage =
          BitmapFactory.decodeStream(imageStream);
            src = new Mat(selectedImage.getHeight(),
                selectedImage.getWidth(), CvType.CV_8UC4);
                    Utils.bitmapToMat(selectedImage, src);

                switch (ACTION_MODE){
                    //Add different cases here depending
                        on the required operation
                }
                    //Code to convert Mat to Bitmap to
                        load in an ImageView. Also load
                        original image in imageView

            } catch (FileNotFoundException e) {
                e.printStackTrace();
            }
        }
        break;
}
```

To apply mean blur to an image, we use the OpenCV provided function `blur()`. We have used a 3 x 3 kernel for this purpose:

```
case HomeActivity.MEAN_BLUR:
Imgproc.blur(src, src, new Size(3,3));
    break;
```

Now we will set this image in an ImageView to see the results of the operation:

```
Bitmap processedImage = Bitmap.createBitmap(src.cols(),
  src.rows(), Bitmap.Config.ARGB_8888);
Utils.matToBitmap(src, processedImage);
ivImage.setImageBitmap(selectedImage);
ivImageProcessed.setImageBitmap(processedImage);
```

Original Image (Left) and Image after applying Mean Blur (Right)

The Gaussian blur method

The Gaussian blur is the most commonly used method of blurring. The Gaussian kernel is obtained using the Gaussian function given as follows:

$$f\left(x\right) = \frac{1}{\sigma\sqrt{2\pi}} e^{-\left(x-\mu\right)^2/\left(2\sigma^2\right)}$$

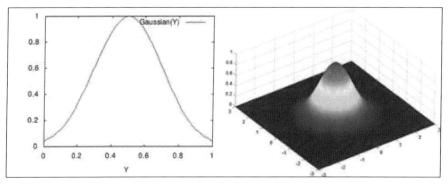

The Gaussian Function in one and two dimensions

The anchor pixel is considered to be at (0, 0). As we can see, the pixels closer to the anchor pixel are given a higher weightage than those further away from it. This is generally the ideal scenario, as the nearby pixels should influence the result of a particular pixel more than those further away. The Gaussian kernels of size 3, 5, and 7 are shown in the following figure (image of 'Gaussian kernels' taken from `http://www1.adept.com/main/KE/DATA/ACE/AdeptSight_User/ImageProcessing_Operations.html`):

These are the Gaussian kernels of size 3 x 3, 5 x 5 and 7 x 7.

To use the Gaussian blur in your application, OpenCV provides a built-in function called **GaussianBlur**. We will use this and get the following resulting image. We will add a new case to the same switch block we used earlier. For this code, declare a constant `GAUSSIAN_BLUR` with value 2:

```
case HomeActivity.GAUSSIAN_BLUR:
    Imgproc.GaussianBlur(src, src, new Size(3,3), 0);
    break;
```

Image after applying Gaussian blur on the original image

The median blur method

One of the common types of noise present in images is called salt-and-pepper noise. In this kind of noise, sparsely occurring black and white pixels are distributed over the image. To remove this type of noise, we use median blur. In this kind of blur, we arrange the pixels covered by our kernel in ascending/descending order, and set the value of the middle element as the final value of the anchor pixel. The advantage of using this type of filtering is that salt-and-pepper noise is sparsely occurring, and so its influence is only over a small number of pixels when averaging their values. Thus, over a bigger area, the number of noise pixels is fewer than the number of pixels that are useful, as shown in the following image:

Example of salt-and-pepper noise

To apply median blur in OpenCV, we use the built-in function `medianBlur`. As in the previous cases, we have to add a button and add the `OnClickListener` functions. We will add another case condition for this operation:

```
case HomeActivity.MEDIAN_BLUR:
    Imgproc.medianBlur(src, src, 3);
    break;
```

Resulting image after applying median blur

[Median blur does not use convolution.]

Creating custom kernels

We have seen how different types of kernels affect the image. What if we want to create our own kernels for different applications that aren't natively offered by OpenCV? In this section, we will see how we can achieve just that. We will try to form a sharper image from a given input.

Sharpening can be thought of as a linear filtering operation where the anchor pixel has a high weightage and the surrounding pixels have a low weightage. A kernel satisfying this constraint is shown in the following table:

0	-1	0
-1	5	-1
0	-1	0

We will use this kernel to perform the convolution on our image:

```
case HomeActivity.SHARPEN:
    Mat kernel = new Mat(3,3,CvType.CV_16SC1);
        kernel.put(0, 0, 0, -1, 0, -1, 5, -1, 0, -1, 0);
```

Here we have given the image depth as `16SC1`. This means that each pixel in our image contains a 16-bit signed integer (16S) and the image has 1 channel (C1).

Now we will use the `filter2D()` function, which performs the actual convolution when given the input image and a kernel. We will show the image in an ImageView. We will add another case to the switch block created earlier:

```
Imgproc.filter2D(src, src, src.depth(), kernel);
```

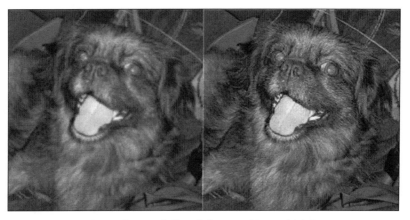

Original image (left) and sharpened image (right)

Morphological operations

Morphological operations are a set of operations that process an image based on the features of the image and a structuring element. These generally work on binary or grayscale images. We will take a look at some basic morphological operations before moving on to more advance ones.

Dilation

Dilation is a method by which the bright regions of an image are expanded. To achieve this, we take a kernel of the desired size and replace the anchor pixel with the maximum value overlapped by the kernel. Dilation can be used to merge objects that might have been broken off.

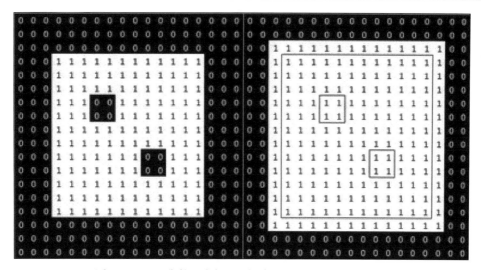

A binary image (left) and the result after applying dilation (right)

To apply this operation, we use the `dilate()` function. We need to use a kernel to perform dilation. We use the `getStructuringElement()` OpenCV function to get the required kernel.

OpenCV provides `MORPH_RECT`, `MORPH_CROSS`, and `MORPH_ELLIPSE` as options to create our required kernels:

```
case HomeActivity.DILATE:
    Mat kernelDilate = Imgproc.getStructuringElement(
      Imgproc.MORPH_RECT, new Size(3, 3));
    Imgproc.dilate(src, src, kernelDilate);
    break;
```

Original image (left) and dilated image (right)

If we use a rectangular structuring element, the image grows in the shape of a rectangle. Similarly, if we use an elliptical structuring element, the image grows in the shape of an ellipse.

Erosion

Similarly, erosion is a method by which the dark regions of an image are expanded. To achieve this, we take a kernel of the desired size and replace the anchor pixel by the minimum value overlapped by the kernel. Erosion can be used to remove the noise from images.

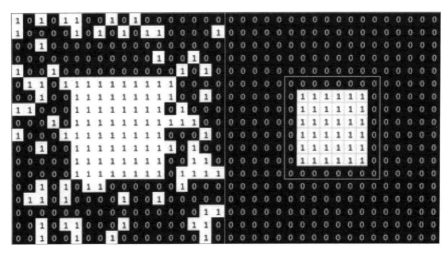

A binary image (left) and the result after applying erosion (right)

To apply this operation, we use the `erode()` function:

```
case HomeActivity.ERODE:
    Mat kernelErode = Imgproc.getStructuringElement(Imgproc.MORPH_
ELLIPSE, new Size(5, 5));
    Imgproc.erode(src, src, kernelErode);
        break;
```

Original image (left) and eroded image (right)

Erosion and dilation are not inverse operations.

Thresholding

Thresholding is the method of segmenting out sections of an image that we would like to analyze. The value of each pixel is compared to a predefined threshold value and based on this result, we modify the value of the pixel. OpenCV provides five types of thresholding operations.

To perform thresholding, we will use the following code as a template and change the parameters as per the kind of thresholding required. We need to replace THRESH_CONSTANT with the constant for the required method of thresholding:

```
case HomeActivity.THRESHOLD:
    Imgproc.threshold(src, src, 100, 255,
      Imgproc.THRESH_CONSTANT);
    break;
```

Here, 100 is the threshold value and 255 is the maximum value (the value of pure white).

The constants are listed in the following table:

Thresholding Method Name	Thresholding Function	Constant
Binary threshold	$dst(x,y) = \begin{cases} maxVal; & \text{if } src(x,y) > thresh \\ 0 & \text{otherwise} \end{cases}$	THRESH_BINARY
Threshold to zero	$dst(x,y) = \begin{cases} src(x,y); & \text{if } src(x,y) > thresh \\ 0; & \text{otherwise} \end{cases}$	THRESH_TOZERO
Truncate	$dst(x,y) = \begin{cases} thresh; & \text{if } src(x,y) > thresh \\ src(x,y); & \text{otherwise} \end{cases}$	THRESH_TRUNC
Binary threshold, inverted	$dst(x,y) = \begin{cases} 0; & \text{if } src(x,y) > thresh \\ maxVal; & \text{otherwise} \end{cases}$	THRESH_BINARY_INV
Threshold to zero, inverted	$dst(x,y) = \begin{cases} 0; & \text{if } src(x,y) > thresh \\ src(x,y); & \text{otherwise} \end{cases}$	THRESH_TOZERO_INV

The following image for thresholding results is taken from `http://docs.opencv.org/trunk/d7/d4d/tutorial_py_thresholding.html`:

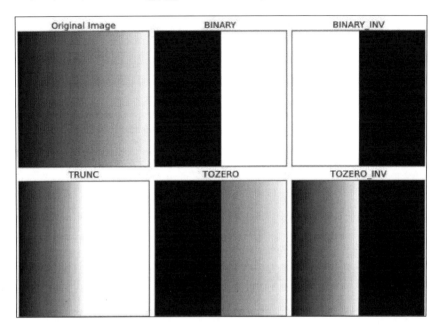

Adaptive thresholding

Setting a global threshold value may not be the best option when performing segmentation. Lighting conditions affect the intensity of pixels. So, to overcome this limitation, we will try to calculate the threshold value for any pixel based on its neighboring pixels.

We will use three parameters to calculate the adaptive threshold of an image:

1. **Adaptive method**: The following are the two methods we will use:
   - `ADAPTIVE_THRESH_MEAN_C`: The threshold value is the mean of the neighboring pixels
   - `ADAPTIVE_THRESH_GAUSSIAN_C`: The threshold value is the weighted sum of the neighboring pixel values, where weights are Gaussian kernels

2. **Block Size**: This is the size of the neighborhood

3. **C**: This is the constant that has to be subtracted from the mean/weighted mean calculated for each pixel:

```
case HomeActivity.ADAPTIVE_THRESHOLD:
    Imgproc.cvtColor(src, src, Imgproc.COLOR_BGR2GRAY);
    Imgproc.adaptiveThreshold(src, src, 255, Imgproc.ADAPTIVE_
THRESH_GAUSSIAN_C,
  Imgproc.THRESH_BINARY, 3, 0);
    break;
```

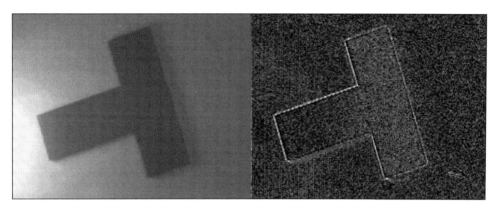

Original image (left) and image after applying Adaptive thresholding (right)

Here, the resulting image has a lot of noise present. This can be avoided by applying a blurring operation before applying adaptive thresholding, so as to smooth the image.

Summary

In this chapter, we have learnt how to get started with using OpenCV in your Android project. Then we looked at different filters in image processing, especially linear filters, and how they can be implemented on an Android device. These filters will later form the basis of any computer vision application that you try to build. In the following chapters, we will look at more complex image filters, and also see how to extract information from the images in the form of edges, corners, and the like.

2

Detecting Basic Features in Images

After reading about the basics of image processing and manipulation in the previous chapter, we will take a look at some of the most widely used algorithms used to extract meaningful information from the images in the form of edges, lines, circles, ellipses, blobs or contours, user defined shapes, and corners. In context of *computer vision* and *image processing*, such information is often termed as *features*. In this chapter, we will take a look at the various feature detection algorithms, such as Edge and Corner detection algorithms, Hough transformations, and Contour detection algorithms and their implementations on an Android platform using OpenCV.

To make our lives simpler, and have a clear understanding of this chapter, we will first create a basic Android application to which we will keep adding implementations of different feature detection algorithms. This will reduce the amount of extra code that we would otherwise have to write for each algorithm in this chapter.

Creating our application

Let's create a very basic Android application that will read images from your phone's gallery and display them on the screen using the *ImageView* control. The application will also have a menu option to open the gallery to choose an image.

We will start off by creating a new Eclipse (or an Android Studio) project with a blank activity, and let's call our application **Features App**.

Before doing anything to the application, initialize OpenCV in your application (refer to *Chapter 1, Applying Effects to Images*, on how to initialize OpenCV in an Android project).

To the blank activity, add an `ImageView` control (used to display the image), as shown in the following code snippet:

```
<ImageView
         android:layout_width="fill_parent"
         android:layout_height="fill_parent"
         android:id="@+id/image_view"
         android:visibility="visible"/>
```

In the application menu, add an `OpenGallery` menu option to open the phone's gallery and help us pick an image. For this, add a new menu item in the project's menu resource XML file (default location of the file is `/res/menu/filename.xml`), as follows:

```
<item android:id="@+id/OpenGallery"
   android:title="@string/OpenGallery"
         android:orderInCategory="100"
           android:showAsAction="never" />
```

For more detailed information on menus in Android, refer to `http://developer.android.com/guide/topics/ui/menus.html`.

Let's now make the `OpenGallery` menu option functional. Android API exposes a `public boolean onOptionsItemSelected(MenuItem item)` function that allows the developer to program the option selection event. In this function, we will add a piece of code that will open the gallery of your phone to choose an image. Android API provides a predefined intent `Intent.ACTION_PICK` just for this task; that is, to open the gallery and pick an image. We will use this intent for our application, as follows:

```
Intent intent = new Intent(Intent.ACTION_PICK,
   Uri.parse("content://media/internal/images/media"));
```

Let's modify the `public boolean onOptionsItemSelected(MenuItem item)` function and make it function as per our need.

The final implementation of the function should look like this:

```
public boolean onOptionsItemSelected(MenuItem item) {
        // Handle action bar item clicks here. The action bar will
        // automatically handle clicks on the Home/Up
          button, so long
        // as you specify a parent activity in
          AndroidManifest.xml.
        int id = item.getItemId();

        //noinspection SimplifiableIfStatement
        if (id == R.id.action_settings) {
           return true;
        }
        else if (id == R.id.open_gallery) {
            Intent intent = new Intent(Intent.ACTION_PICK,
              Uri.parse("content://media/internal/images/media"));
            startActivityForResult(intent, 0);
        }
    }
```

This code has nothing but a bunch of easy-to-understand if else statements. The thing you need to understand here is the `startActivityForResult()` function. As you might have realized, we want to bring the image data from `ACTION_PICK Intent` in to our application so that we can use it later as an input for our feature detection algorithms. For this reason, instead of using the `startActivity()` function, we use `startActivityForResult()`. After the user is done with the subsequent activity, the system calls the `onActivityResult()` function along with the result from the called intent, which is the gallery picker in our case. Our work now is to implement the `onActivityResult()` function in accordance with our application. Let's first enumerate what we want to do with the returned image. Not much actually; correct the orientation of the image and display it on the screen using `ImageView` that we added to our activity in the beginning of this section.

You must be wondering what is meant by correcting the orientation of an image. In any Android phone, there can be multiple sources of images, such as the native camera application, the Java camera app, or any other third-party app. Each of them might have different ways of capturing and storing images. Now, in your application, when you load these images, it may so happen that they are rotated by some angle. Before these images can be used in our application, we should correct their orientation so that they appear meaningful to your application users. We will take a look at the code to do this now.

The following is the onActivityResult() function for our application:

```
protected void onActivityResult(int requestCode,
  int resultCode, Intent data) {
      super.onActivityResult(requestCode, resultCode, data);

      if (requestCode == 0 && resultCode == RESULT_OK &&
        null != data) {
          Uri selectedImage = data.getData();
          String[] filePathColumn =
            {MediaStore.Images.Media.DATA};

          Cursor cursor =
            getContentResolver().query(selectedImage,
                filePathColumn, null, null, null);
          cursor.moveToFirst();

          int columnIndex =
            cursor.getColumnIndex(filePathColumn[0]);
          String picturePath = cursor.getString(columnIndex);
          cursor.close();

          // String picturePath contains the path
            of selected Image

          //To speed up loading of image
          BitmapFactory.Options options = new
            BitmapFactory.Options();
          options.inSampleSize = 2;

          Bitmap temp =
            BitmapFactory.decodeFile(picturePath, options);

          //Get orientation information
          int orientation = 0;
          try {
              ExifInterface imgParams = new
                ExifInterface(picturePath);
              orientation =
                imgParams.getAttributeInt(
                ExifInterface.TAG_ORIENTATION,
                ExifInterface.ORIENTATION_UNDEFINED);

          } catch (IOException e) {
```

```
                    e.printStackTrace();
            }


            //Rotating the image to get the correct orientation
            Matrix rotate90 = new Matrix();
            rotate90.postRotate(orientation);
            originalBitmap = rotateBitmap(temp,orientation);

            //Convert Bitmap to Mat
            Bitmap tempBitmap =
               originalBitmap.copy(Bitmap.Config.ARGB_8888,true);
            originalMat = new Mat(tempBitmap.getHeight(),
               tempBitmap.getWidth(), CvType.CV_8U);
            Utils.bitmapToMat(tempBitmap, originalMat);

            currentBitmap =
               originalBitmap.copy(Bitmap.Config.ARGB_8888,false);
            loadImageToImageView();
        }
    }
```

Let's see what this long piece of code does. First, we do a sanity check and see whether the result is coming from the appropriate intent (that is, the gallery picker) by checking requestCode and resultCode. After this is done, we try to retrieve the path of the image in your phone's filesystem. From the ACTION.PICK intent, we get the Uri of the selected image, which we will store in Uri selectedImage. To get the exact path of the image, we make use of the Cursor class. We initialize a new Cursor class object with it pointing toward our selectedImage. Using MediaStore. Images.Media.DATA, we fetch the column index of the selected image, and then eventually, the path of the image using the cursor class declared earlier, and store it in a string, picturePath. After we have the path of the image, we create a new Bitmap object temp to store the image. So far, we have been able to read the image and store it in a bitmap object. Next we need to correct the orientation. For this, we first extract the orientation information from the image using the ExifInterface class. As you can see in the code, the ExifInterface class gives us the orientation information through ExifInterface.TAG_ORIENTATION. Using this orientation information, we rotate our bitmap accordingly using the rotateBitmap() function.

 For implementation of the rotateBitmap() function, refer to the code bundle that accompanies this book.

After correcting the orientation, we make two copies of the bitmap: one to store the original image (`originalBitmap`) and the other one to store the processed bitmaps (`currentBitmap`), that is, to store the outputs of different algorithms applied to the original bitmap. The only part left is to display the image on the screen. Create a new function `loadImageToView()` and add the following lines to it:

```
private void loadImageToImageView()
{
        ImageView imgView = (ImageView) findViewById(R.id.image_view);
        imgView.setImageBitmap(currentBitmap);
}
```

The first line creates an instance of `ImageView` and the second line sets that image onto the view. Simple!

One last thing and our application is ready! Since our application is going to read data from permanent storage (read images from external storage), we need permission. To the `AndroidManifest.xml` file, add the following lines that will allow the application to access external storage for reading data:

```
<uses-permission
    android:name="android.permission.READ_EXTERNAL_STORAGE"/>
```

Now that we have our basic application in place, let's take a look at the different feature detection algorithms, starting with Edge and Corner detection, Hough transformation, and Contours.

Edge and Corner detection

Edge detection and Corner detection are two of the most basic feature detection algorithms, and are very useful ones too. Having information about the edges in an image can be of great help in applications, where you want to find boundaries of different objects in an image, or you need to find corners in an image when you want to analyze how an object rotates or moves in a given sequence of images (or videos). In this section, we will take a look at the techniques and implementations of various Edge and Corner detection algorithms, such as Difference of Gaussian, Canny Edge detector, Sobel Operator, and Harris Corners.

The Difference of Gaussian technique

Let's start with the easiest and the most rudimentary technique. Before we understand how **Difference of Gaussian (DoG)** works, let's take a look at what exactly edges are. To put it simply, edges are points in an image where the pixel intensity changes appreciably. We will exploit this property of edges and by applying Gaussian blur on the image, we will compute the edge points (Edges).

Here is a three-step explanation of the algorithm:

1. Convert the given image to a grayscale image.

2. On the grayscale image, perform Gaussian blur using two different blurring radiuses (you should have two Gaussian blurred images after this step).

3. Subtract (arithmetic subtraction) the two images generated in the previous step to get the resultant image with only edge points (Edges) in it.

Why does this technique work? How can subtracting two Gaussian blurred images give us edge points? A Gaussian filter is used to smooth out an image and the extent of smoothening depends on the blurring radius. Consider an image of a chess board. When you apply a Gaussian filter to the chess board image, you will observe that there is almost no change near the center of the white and black squares, whereas the common side of the black and white squares (which is an edge point) gets smudged, implying loss of edge information. Gaussian blur makes the edge less prominent.

According to our technique, we have two Gaussian blurred images with different blurring radius. When you subtract these two images, you will lose all the points where no smoothening or smudging happened, that is, the center of the black and white squares in the case of a chess board image. However, pixel values near the edges would have changed because smudging pixel values and subtracting such points will give us a non-zero value, indicating an edge point. Hence, you get edge points after subtracting two Gaussian blurred images.

Since we are only performing Gaussian blurs on images, it is one of the fastest ways of calculating edges. Having said that, it is also true that this technique does not return very promising results. This technique might work very well for some images and can completely fail in some scenarios. However, it doesn't hurt to know one extra algorithm!

Let's modify our Features App that we created in the last section and apply DoG to it. In the applications menu, we add a new menu option, *Difference of Gaussian*, to the menu resource XML file using these lines:

```
<item android:id="@+id/DoG" android:title="@string/DoG"
        android:orderInCategory="100"
          android:showAsAction="never" />
```

Make a new function public void DifferenceOfGaussian(), which will compute edges in any given image, as follows:

```
public void DifferenceOfGaussian()
    {
        Mat grayMat = new Mat();
        Mat blur1 = new Mat();
        Mat blur2 = new Mat();

        //Converting the image to grayscale
        Imgproc.cvtColor(originalMat
          ,grayMat,Imgproc.COLOR_BGR2GRAY);

        //Bluring the images using two different blurring radius
        Imgproc.GaussianBlur(grayMat,blur1,new Size(15,15),5);
        Imgproc.GaussianBlur(grayMat,blur2,new Size(21,21),5);

        //Subtracting the two blurred images
        Mat DoG = new Mat();
        Core.absdiff(blur1, blur2,DoG);

        //Inverse Binary Thresholding
        Core.multiply(DoG,new Scalar(100), DoG);
        Imgproc.threshold(DoG,DoG,50,255
          ,Imgproc.THRESH_BINARY_INV);

        //Converting Mat back to Bitmap
        Utils.matToBitmap(DoG, currentBitmap);
        loadImageToImageView();
    }
```

In the preceding piece of code, we first convert the image to a grayscale image. Then, we apply the Gaussian filter to the image twice, with two different blurring radiuses, using the `Imgproc.GaussianBlur()` function. The first and second parameters in this function are input and output images, respectively. The third parameter specifies the size of the kernel to be used while applying the filter, and the last parameter specifies the value of sigma used in the Gaussian function. Then we determine the absolute difference of the images using `Core.absdiff()`. Once this is done, we post-process our image to make it comprehensible by applying the *Inverse Binary Threshold* operation to set the edge point values to white (255). Finally, we convert the bitmap to Mat and display it on the screen using `loadImageToView()`.

Here is the resulting image after applying DoG on Lenna:

Difference of Gaussian is not often used because it has been superseded by other more sophisticated techniques that we are going to discuss later in this chapter.

The Canny Edge detector

Canny Edge detection is a widely used algorithm in computer vision and is often considered as an optimal technique for edge detection. The algorithm uses more sophisticated techniques than Difference of Gaussian, such as intensity gradient in multiple directions, and thresholding with hysteresis.

The algorithm is broadly divided into four stages:

1. **Smoothing the image**: This is the first step of the algorithm, where we reduce the amount of noise present in the image by performing a Gaussian blur with an appropriate blurring radius.

2. **Calculating the gradient of the image**: Here we calculate the intensity gradient of the image and classify the gradients as vertical, horizontal, or diagonal. The output of this step is used to calculate actual edges in the next stage.

3. **Non-maximal supression**: Using the direction of gradient calculated in the previous step, we check whether or not a pixel is the local maxima in the positive and negative direction of the gradient if not then, we suppress the pixel (which means that a pixel is not a part of any edge). This is an edge thinning technique. Select edge points with the sharpest change.

4. **Edge selection through hysteresis thresholding**: This is the final step of the algorithm. Here we check whether an edge is strong enough to be included in the final output, essentially removing all the less prominent edges.

 Refer to `http://en.wikipedia.org/wiki/Canny_edge_detector` for a more detailed explanation.

The following is an implementation of the algorithm using OpenCV for Android.

For Difference of Gaussian, first add the *Canny Edges* option to the application menu by adding a new item in the menu resource XML file, as follows:

```
<item android:id="@+id/CannyEdges"
  android:title="@string/CannyEdges"
      android:orderInCategory="100"
        android:showAsAction="never" />
```

Create a new function, `public void Canny()`, and add the following lines of code to it:

```
//Canny Edge Detection
    public void Canny()
    {
        Mat grayMat = new Mat();
        Mat cannyEdges = new Mat();
        //Converting the image to grayscale
            Imgproc.cvtColor(originalMat,grayMat,Imgproc.COLOR_
BGR2GRAY);

        Imgproc.Canny(grayMat, cannyEdges,10, 100);

        //Converting Mat back to Bitmap
        Utils.matToBitmap(cannyEdges, currentBitmap);
        loadImageToImageView();
    }
```

In the preceding code, we first convert our image to a grayscale image, and then simply call the `Imgproc.Canny()` function implemented in the OpenCV API for Android. The important thing to notice here are the last two parameters in `Imgproc.Canny()`. They are for low and high thresholds respectively. In Canny Edge detection algorithm, we classify each point in the image into one of three classes, `suppressed points`, `weak edge points`, and `strong edge points`. All the points that have the intensity gradient value less than the low threshold values are classified as suppressed points, points with the intensity gradient value between low and high threshold values are classified as weak edge points, and points with the intensity gradient value above the high threshold values are classified as strong edge points.

According to the algorithm, we ignore all the suppressed points. They will not be a part of any edge in the image. Strong edge points definitely form a part of an edge. For weak edge points, we check whether they are connected to any strong edge points in the image by checking the eight pixels around that weak point. If there are any strong edge points in those eight pixels, we count that weak point as a part of the edge. That's Canny Edge detection!

The Sobel operator

Another technique for computing edges in an image is using the Sobel operator (or Sobel filter). As in Canny Edge detection, we calculate the intensity gradient of the pixel, but in a different way. Here we calculate the approximate intensity gradient by convoluting the image with two 3x3 kernels for horizontal and vertical directions each:

-1	0	+1
-2	0	+2
-1	0	+1

x filter

+1	+2	+1
0	0	0
-1	-2	-1

y filter

Convolution matrices used in Sobel filter

Using the horizontal and vertical gradient values, we calculate the absolute gradient at each pixel using this formula:

$$|G| = \sqrt{Gx^2 + Gy^2}$$

For an approximate gradient, the following formula is usually used:

$$|G| = |Gx| + |Gy|$$

The steps involved in computing edges using a Sobel operator are as follows:

1. Convert the image to a grayscale image.
2. Calculate the absolute value of the intensity gradient in the horizontal direction.
3. Calculate the absolute value of the intensity gradient in the vertical direction.
4. Compute the resultant gradient using the preceding formula.
   The resultant gradient values are essentially the edges.

Let's now add a Sobel filter to our Features App. Start by adding a *Sobel filter* menu option in the menu's XML file:

```xml
<item android:id="@+id/SobelFilter"
  android:title="@string/SobelFilter"
        android:orderInCategory="100"
          android:showAsAction="never" />
```

The following is a Sobel filter using OpenCV for Android:

```java
//Sobel Operator
    void Sobel()
    {
        Mat grayMat = new Mat();
        Mat sobel = new Mat(); //Mat to store the result

        //Mat to store gradient and absolute gradient respectively
        Mat grad_x = new Mat();
        Mat abs_grad_x = new Mat();

        Mat grad_y = new Mat();
        Mat abs_grad_y = new Mat();

        //Converting the image to grayscale
        Imgproc.cvtColor(originalMat
          ,grayMat,Imgproc.COLOR_BGR2GRAY);

        //Calculating gradient in horizontal direction
        Imgproc.Sobel(grayMat, grad_x,CvType.CV_16S, 1,0,3,1,0);

        //Calculating gradient in vertical direction
        Imgproc.Sobel(grayMat, grad_y,CvType.CV_16S, 0,1,3,1,0);

        //Calculating absolute value of
          gradients in both the direction
        Core.convertScaleAbs(grad_x, abs_grad_x);
        Core.convertScaleAbs(grad_y, abs_grad_y);

        //Calculating the resultant gradient
        Core.addWeighted(abs_grad_x, 0.5,
          abs_grad_y, 0.5, 1, sobel);

        //Converting Mat back to Bitmap
        Utils.matToBitmap(sobel, currentBitmap);
        loadImageToImageView();
    }
```

In this code, we first convert the image to a grayscale image. After this, using the grayscale image, we calculate the intensity gradient in the horizontal and vertical directions using the `Imgproc.Sobel()` function, and store the output in `grad_x` and `grad_y`. As per the formula mentioned in the algorithm, we calculate the absolute value of the gradients and add them together to get the resultant gradient value (basically the edges). The following code snippet performs the described step:

```
//Calculating absolute value of gradients in both the direction
        Core.convertScaleAbs(grad_x, abs_grad_x);
        Core.convertScaleAbs(grad_y, abs_grad_y);

        //Calculating the resultant gradient
        Core.addWeighted(abs_grad_x,
          0.5, abs_grad_y, 0.5, 1, sobel);
```

Finally, we convert the Mat into a bitmap and display it on the screen.

> You may also be interested to take a look at the Prewitt operator (http://en.wikipedia.org/wiki/Prewitt_operator). It is similar to a Sobel operator, but uses a different matrix for convolution.

Harris Corner detection

In the literal sense of the term, corners are points of intersection of two edges or a point which has multiple prominent edge directions in its local neighborhood. Corners are often considered as points of interest in an image and are used in many applications, ranging from image correlation, video stabilization, 3D modelling, and the likes. Harris Corner detection is one of the most used techniques in corner detection; and in this section, we will take a look at how to implement it on an Android platform.

Harris corner detector uses a sliding window over the image to calculate the variation in intensity. Since corners will have large variations in the intensity values around them, we are looking for positions in the image where the sliding windows show large variations in intensity. We try to maximize the following term:

$$\sum \left[I\left(x+u, y+v\right) - I\left(x, y\right) \right]^2$$

Here, **I** is the image, **u** is the shift in the sliding window in the horizontal direction, and **v** is the shift in the vertical direction.

The following is an implementation of Harris Corner using OpenCV:

```
void HarrisCorner() {
        Mat grayMat = new Mat();
        Mat corners = new Mat();

        //Converting the image to grayscale
        Imgproc.cvtColor(originalMat, grayMat,
          Imgproc.COLOR_BGR2GRAY);

        Mat tempDst = new Mat();
        //finding corners          Imgproc.cornerHarris(grayMat,
          tempDst, 2, 3, 0.04);

        //Normalizing harris corner's output
        Mat tempDstNorm = new Mat();
        Core.normalize(tempDst, tempDstNorm,
          0, 255, Core.NORM_MINMAX);
        Core.convertScaleAbs(tempDstNorm, corners);

        //Drawing corners on a new image
        Random r = new Random();
        for (int i = 0; i < tempDstNorm.cols(); i++) {
            for (int j = 0; j < tempDstNorm.rows(); j++) {
                double[] value = tempDstNorm.get(j, i);
                if (value[0] > 150)
                    Core.circle(corners, new Point(i, j),
                       5, new Scalar(r.nextInt(255)), 2);
            }
        }

        //Converting Mat back to Bitmap
        Utils.matToBitmap(corners, currentBitmap);
        loadImageToImageView();
    }
```

In the preceding code, we start off by converting the image to a grayscale image and then use it as an input to the `Imgproc.cornerHarris()` function. The other inputs to the function are the block size, kernel size, and a parameter, k, that is used to solve one of the equations in the algorithm (for details on mathematics, refer to OpenCV's documentation on Harris Corner at `http://docs.opencv.org/doc/tutorials/ features2d/trackingmotion/harris_detector/harris_detector.html`). The output of Harris Corner is a 16-bit scalar image, which is normalized to get the pixel values in the range 0 to 255. After this, we run a `for` loop and draw all the circles on the image with the centers being points whose intensity value is greater than a certain user set threshold.

Hough transformations

So far, we looked at how to detect edges and corners in an image. Sometimes, for image analysis apart from edges and corners, you want to detect shapes, such as lines, circles, ellipses, or any other shape for that matter. Say for example, you want to detect coins in an image, or you want to detect a box or a grid in an image. A technique that comes handy in such scenarios is Hough transformations. It is a widely used technique that detects shapes in an image using their mathematical equations in their parameterized forms.

The generalized Hough transformation is capable of detecting any shape for which we can provide an equation in the parameterized form. As the shapes start getting complex (with an increase in the number of dimensions), such as spheres or ellipsoids, it gets computationally expensive; hence, we generally look at standard Hough transformations for simple 2D shapes, such as lines and circles.

In this section, we will take a look at Hough transformations to detect lines and circles, but as mentioned earlier, it can be further extended to detect shapes, such as ellipses, and even simple 3D shapes, such as spheres.

Hough lines

Detecting lines is one of the simplest use cases of Hough transformations. In Hough lines, we select a pair of points from our image *(x1, y1)* and *(x2, y2)*, and solve the following pair of equations for *(a, m)*:

y1 = m(x1) + a

y2 = m(x2) + a

We maintain a table with two columns *(a, m)* and a count value. The count value keeps a record of how many times we get the *(a, m)* value after solving the preceding pair of equations. This is nothing but a voting procedure. After calculating the *(a, m)* values for all possible pairs of points, we take the *(a, m)* values that have count values greater than a certain threshold and these values are the desired lines in the image.

For Hough transformations, we never run the algorithm directly on the image. First, we compute the edges in the image, and then apply the Hough transformation on the edges. The reason being, any prominent line in the image has to be an edge (the reverse is not true, every edge in the image will not be a line), and using only edges, we are reducing the number of points on which the algorithm runs.

OpenCV provides two implementations of Hough lines: standard Hough lines and probabilistic Hough lines. The major difference between the two is that, in probabilistic Hough lines, instead of using all edge points, we select a subset of the edge points by random sampling. This makes the algorithm run faster since there are fewer points to deal with, without compromising on its performance.

Time to write some code! First things first, add a new *Hough lines* menu option to our application menu. However, try to figure out the code to do this yourself this time.

Hopefully, the menu option is now in place! Let's now take a look at a code snippet that uses the probabilistic Hough transformation to detect lines in an image using OpenCV for Android:

```
void HoughLines()
    {

        Mat grayMat = new Mat();
        Mat cannyEdges = new Mat();
        Mat lines = new Mat();

        //Converting the image to grayscale
        Imgproc.cvtColor(originalMat
          ,grayMat,Imgproc.COLOR_BGR2GRAY);

        Imgproc.Canny(grayMat, cannyEdges,10, 100);

        Imgproc.HoughLinesP(cannyEdges,
          lines, 1, Math.PI/180, 50, 20, 20);

        Mat houghLines = new Mat();
        houghLines.create(cannyEdges.rows(),
          cannyEdges.cols(),CvType.CV_8UC1);
```

```
//Drawing lines on the image
for(int i = 0 ; i < lines.cols() ; i++)
{
    double[] points = lines.get(0,i);
    double x1, y1, x2, y2;

    x1 = points[0];
    y1 = points[1];
    x2 = points[2];
    y2 = points[3];

    Point pt1 = new Point(x1, y1);
    Point pt2 = new Point(x2, y2);

    //Drawing lines on an image
    Core.line(houghLines, pt1, pt2,
      new Scalar(255, 0, 0), 1);
}

//Converting Mat back to Bitmap
Utils.matToBitmap(houghLines, currentBitmap);
loadImageToImageView();

}
```

As explained earlier, we first compute edges in the image using any edge detection technique (the preceding code uses Canny). The output of the Canny Edge detector is used as an input to the `Imgproc.HoughLinesP()` function. The first and second parameters are input and output respectively. The third and fourth parameters specify the resolution of r and theta in pixels. The next two parameters are the threshold and minimum number of points that a line should have. Lines with fewer points than this are discarded.

The `For` loop in the code is used to draw all the lines on the image. This is only done to visualize the lines detected by the algorithm.

Hough circles

Analogous to Hough lines, Hough circles also follow the same procedure to detect circles, only the equations change (the parameterized form of a circle is used instead).

Here is an implementation of Hough circles using OpenCV for Android:

```java
void HoughCircles()
{
    Mat grayMat = new Mat();
    Mat cannyEdges = new Mat();
    Mat circles = new Mat();

    //Converting the image to grayscale
    Imgproc.cvtColor(originalMat
      ,grayMat,Imgproc.COLOR_BGR2GRAY);

    Imgproc.Canny(grayMat, cannyEdges,10, 100);

    Imgproc.HoughCircles(cannyEdges, circles,
      Imgproc.CV_HOUGH_GRADIENT,1, cannyEdges.rows() / 15);
      //, grayMat.rows() / 8);

    Mat houghCircles = new Mat();
    houghCircles.create(cannyEdges.rows(),cannyEdges.cols()
      ,CvType.CV_8UC1);

    //Drawing lines on the image
    for(int i = 0 ; i < circles.cols() ; i++)
    {
        double[] parameters = circles.get(0,i);
        double x, y;
        int r;

        x = parameters[0];
        y = parameters[1];
        r = (int)parameters[2];

        Point center = new Point(x, y);

        //Drawing circles on an image
        Core.circle(houghCircles,center,r,
          new Scalar(255,0,0),1);
    }

    //Converting Mat back to Bitmap
    Utils.matToBitmap(houghCircles, currentBitmap);
    loadImageToImageView();
}
```

The code is pretty much the same as Hough lines with a few changes. The output of `Imgproc.HoughCircles()` is a tuple of center coordinates and the radius of the circle (x, y, radius). To draw circles on the image, we use `Core.circle()`.

 A nice coding exercise would be to implement Hough lines/circles without using the predefined OpenCV functions.

Contours

We are often required to break down the image into smaller segments to have a more focused view of the object of interest. Say for instance, you have an image with balls from different sports, such as a golf ball, cricket ball, tennis ball, and football. However, you are only interested in analyzing the football. One way of doing this could be by using Hough circles that we looked at in the last section. Another way of doing this is using contour detection to segment the image into smaller parts, with each segment representing a particular ball.

The next step is to choose the segment having the largest area, that is, your football (it is safe to assume that the football would be the largest of all!).

Contours are nothing but connected curves in an image or boundaries of connected components in an image. Contours are often computed using edges in an image, but a subtle difference between edges and contours is that contours are closed, whereas edges can be anything. The concept of edges is very local to the point and its neighboring pixels; however, contours take care of the object as a whole (they return boundaries of objects).

Let's take a look at the implementation of Contour detection using OpenCV for Android. Let's take a look at the following code:

```
void Contours()
    {
        Mat grayMat = new Mat();
        Mat cannyEdges = new Mat();
        Mat hierarchy = new Mat();

        List<MatOfPoint> contourList = new
          ArrayList<MatOfPoint>();
          //A list to store all the contours
```

```
//Converting the image to grayscale
Imgproc.cvtColor(originalMat,grayMat
  ,Imgproc.COLOR_BGR2GRAY);

Imgproc.Canny(grayMat, cannyEdges,10, 100);

//finding contours
Imgproc.findContours(cannyEdges,contourList
  ,hierarchy,Imgproc.RETR_LIST,
    Imgproc.CHAIN_APPROX_SIMPLE);

//Drawing contours on a new image
Mat contours = new Mat();
contours.create(cannyEdges.rows()
    ,cannyEdges.cols(),CvType.CV_8UC3);
Random r = new Random();
for(int i = 0; i < contourList.size(); i++)
{
    Imgproc.drawContours(contours
        ,contourList,i,new Scalar(r.nextInt(255)
        ,r.nextInt(255),r.nextInt(255)), -1);
}
//Converting Mat back to Bitmap
Utils.matToBitmap(contours, currentBitmap);
loadImageToImageView();
}
```

OpenCV does make our life simple! In this code, we first convert our image to a grayscale image (it is not necessary to use the grayscale version of the image, you can directly work with colored images as well), and then find edges in it using Canny Edge detection. After we have the edges with us, we pass this image to a predefined function `Imgproc.findContours()`. The output of this function is `List<MatOfPoint>` which stores all the contours computed in that image. The parameters passed in to the `Imgproc.findContours()` function are interesting. The first and the second parameters are the input images and list of contours respectively. The third and the fourth parameters are interesting; they give the hierarchy of contours in the image. The third parameter stores the hierarchy, while the fourth parameter specifies the nature of hierarchy the users want. The hierarchy essentially tells us the overall arrangement of contours in the image.

Refer to http://docs.opencv.org/trunk/doc/py_tutorials/ py_imgproc/py_contours/py_contours_hierarchy/py_ contours_hierarchy.html for a detailed explanation of hierarchies in Contours.

The for loop in the code is used to draw contours on a new image. The Imgproc. drawContours() function draws the contours on the image. In this function, the first parameter is a Mat, for where you want to draw the contours. The second parameter is the list of contours returned by Imgproc.findContours(). The third parameter is the index of the contour that we want to draw, and the fourth parameter is the color to be used to draw the contour. While drawing contours, you have two options: either you draw the boundary of the contour or you fill the entire contour. The fifth parameter in the function helps you to specify your choice. A negative value means you need to fill the entire contour, whereas any positive value specifies the thickness of the boundary.

Finally, convert Mat to Bitmap and display it on the screen.

With contour detection, we successfully completed our Features App.

Project – detecting a Sudoku puzzle in an image

Let's try to apply our learning from this chapter and create a simple application for detecting a Sudoku grid in an image. You see Sudoku puzzles every day in newspapers or magazines; sometimes they provide a solution and sometimes they don't. Why not build an application for your mobile phone that can click a picture of the Sudoku, analyze the numbers, run some intelligent algorithms to solve the puzzle, and within seconds, you have the solution on your mobile screen.

After reading this chapter, we can easily work on the first part of the application; that is, localizing (detecting) the Sudoku grid from an image. As you read through this book, you will come across algorithms and techniques that will help you build the other parts of this application.

Let's break down our problem statement into subproblems and work each one out to have a fully functioning Sudoku localizing application:

- Capture the image using a camera or load it from your gallery.

- Preprocess the image by running your favorite edge detection algorithm.

- Find a rectangular grid in the image. The possible options are to use Hough lines to detect lines and then look for four lines that form a rectangle (a little tedious), or find contours in the image and assume the largest contours in your image to be the Sudoku grid that you were looking for (the assumption made here is safe providing you click or load a picture that focuses on the grid more than anything else).

- After you have narrowed down on the grid, create a new image and copy only the contour region to the new image.

- You have successfully detected the Sudoku grid!

Here is a sample image with a Sudoku grid in it:

How to solve sudoku puzzles

To solve a sudoku, you only need logic and patience. No math is required.

Simply make sure that each 3x3 square region has a number 1 through 9 with only one occurrence of each number.

Each column and row of the large grid must have only one instance of the numbers 1 through 9.

The difficulty rating on this puzzle is medium.

Answer on p.28

Turkey Time Sudoku

				3		8		2
	3	6				4	1	
8							5	6
5	8							
7			9		2			1
							9	3
1	2							5
	9	7				1	2	
3		8		6				

Here is the narrowed down grid:

Turkey Time Sudoku								
				3		8		2
	3	6				4	1	
8							5	6
5	8							
7			9		2			1
							9	3
1	2							5
	9	7				1	2	
3		8		6				

 This chapter covers everything that one should know about in order to create this application. Once you have tried doing it by yourself, you can download the code from the Packt Publishing website.

Summary

In this chapter, we have learnt about some basic features in images, such as edges, corners, lines, and circles. We have looked at different algorithms, such as Canny Edge detection and Harris corners, that can be implemented on an Android device. These are the basic set of algorithms that will come handy in many applications that we are going to build in the coming chapters.

3
Detecting Objects

One of the common applications of computer vision is to detect objects in an image or video. For example, we can use this method to detect a particular book in a heap of many books. One of the methods to detect objects is **feature matching**. In this chapter, we will learn the following topics:

- What are features?
- Feature detection, description, and matching in images
- SIFT detector and descriptor
- SURF detector and descriptor
- ORB detector and descriptor
- BRISK detector and descriptor
- FREAK descriptor

What are features?

Features are specific patterns that are unique and can be easily tracked and compared. Good features are those that can be distinctly localized. The following image shows the different kind of features:

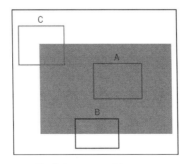

Explains types of features

In the preceding image, patch A is a flat area and is difficult to locate precisely. If we move the rectangle anywhere within the box, the patch contents remain the same. Patch B, being along an edge, is a slightly better feature because if you move it perpendicular to the edge, it changes. However, if you move it parallel to the edge, it is identical to the initial patch. Thus, we can localize these kind of features in at least one dimension. Patch C, being a corner, is a good feature because on moving the rectangle in any direction, the contents of the patch change and can be easily localized. Thus, good features are those which can be easily localized and thus are easy to track.

In the previous chapters, we have seen some of the edge and corner detection algorithms. In this chapter, we will take a look at some more algorithms by which we can find features. This is called **feature detection**. Just detecting features is not enough. We need to be able to differentiate one feature from the other. Hence, we use **feature description** to describe the detected features. The descriptions enable us to find similar features in other images, thereby enabling us to identify objects. Features can also be used to align images and to stitch them together. We will take a look at these applications in the later chapters of this book.

Now we will take a look at some common algorithms available to detect features, such as SIFT, SURF, BRIEF, FAST, and BRISK.

Note that SIFT and SURF are patented algorithms and hence, their free use is only limited to academic and research purposes. For any commercial use of these algorithms, you need to abide by the patent rules and regulations, or speak to the concerned personal.

Scale Invariant Feature Transform

Scale Invariant Feature Transform (**SIFT**) is one of the most widely recognized feature detection algorithms. It was proposed by David Lowe in 2004.

Link to the paper: `http://www.cs.ubc.ca/~lowe/papers/ijcv04.pdf`

Some of the properties of SIFT are as follows:

- It is invariant to scaling and rotation changes in objects
- It is also partially invariant to 3D viewpoint and illumination changes
- A large number of keypoints (features) can be extracted from a single image

Understanding how SIFT works

SIFT follows a strategy of matching robust local features. It is divided into four parts:

- Scale-space extrema detection
- Keypoint localization
- Orientation assignment
- Keypoint descriptor

Scale-space extrema detection

In this step, an image is progressively blurred out using Gaussian blur to get rid of some details in the images. It has been mathematically proven (under reasonable assumptions) that performing Gaussian blur is the only way to carry this out effectively.

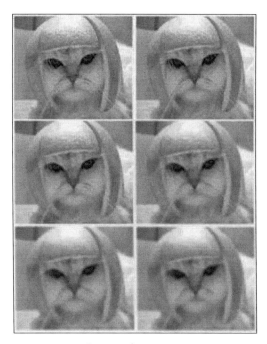

Images of one octave

Progressively blurred images constitute an octave. A new octave is formed by resizing the original image of the previous octave to half and then progressively blurring it. Lowe recommends that you use four octaves of five images each for the best results.

Thus, we see that the images in the first octave are formed by progressively blurring the original image. The first image of the second octave is obtained by resizing the original image in the first octave. Other images in the second octave are formed by the progressive blurring of the first image in the second octave, and so on.

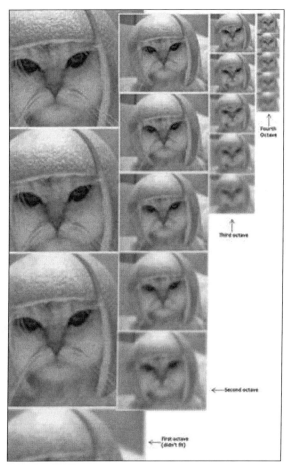

Images of all octaves

To precisely detect edges in an image, we use the Laplacian operator. In this method, second we blur the image a little and then calculate its second derivative. This locates the edges and corners that are good for finding the keypoints. This operation is called the Laplacian of Gaussian.

The second order derivative is extremely sensitive to noise. The blur helps in smoothing out the noise and in stabilizing the second order derivative. The problem is that calculating all these second order derivatives is computationally expensive. So, we cheat a bit:

$$D(x, y, \sigma) = (G(x, y, k\sigma) - G(x, y, \sigma)) * I(x, y)$$

$$= L(x, y, k\sigma) = L(x, y, \sigma)$$

Here, k is a constant multiplicative factor, which represents the amount of blurring in each image in the scale space. A scale space represents the set of images that have been either scaled-up or scaled-down for the purpose of computing keypoints. For example, as shown in the following figure, there are two sets of images: one set is the original set of five images that have been blurred with different blurring radius and another set of scaled down images. The different parameter values can be seen in the following table:

	Scale				
Octave	0.707107	1.000000	1.414214	2.000000	2.828427
	1.414214	2.000000	2.828427	4.000000	5.656854
	2.828427	4.000000	5.656854	8.000000	11.313708
	5.656854	8.000000	11.313708	16.000000	22.627417

To generate the Laplacian of Gaussian images, we calculate the difference between two consecutive images in an octave. This is called the **Difference of Gaussian (DoG)**. These DoG images are approximately equal to those obtained by calculating the Laplacian of Gaussian. Using DoG also has an added benefit. The images obtained are also scale invariant.

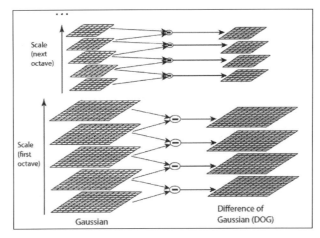

Difference of Gaussian

Using the Laplacian of Gaussian is not only computationally expensive, but it also depends on the amount of blur applied. This is taken care of in the DoG images as a result of normalization.

Keypoint localization

Now these images have been sufficiently preprocessed to enable us to find local extremas. To locate keypoints, we need to iterate over each pixel and compare it with all its neighbors. Instead of just comparing the eight neighbors in that image, we compare the value with its neighbors in that image and also with the images above and below it in that octave, which have nine pixels each:

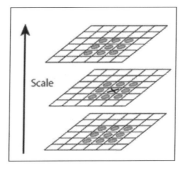

Keypoint localization

So, we can see that we compare a pixel's value with its **26 neighbors**. A pixel is a keypoint if it is the minimum or the maximum among all its 26 neighbors. Usually, a non-maxima or a non-minima doesn't have to go through all 26 comparisons as we may have found its result within a few comparisons.

We do not calculate the keypoints in the uppermost and lowermost images in an octave because we do not have enough neighbors to identify the extremas.

Most of the time, the extremas are never located at the exact pixels. They may be present in between the pixels, but we have no way to access this information in an image. The keypoints located are just their average positions. We use the Taylor series expansion of the scale space function $D(x, y, \sigma)$ (up to the quadratic term) shifted till the current point as origin gives us:

$$D(x) = D + \frac{\partial D^T}{\partial x} x + \frac{1}{2} x^T \frac{\partial^2 D}{\partial x^2} x$$

Here, D and its derivatives are calculated at the point we are currently testing for extrema. Using this formula, by differentiating and equating the result to zero, we can easily find the subpixel keypoint locations:

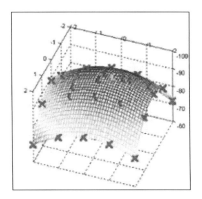

Subpixel extrema localization

SIFT recommends that you generate two such extrema images. Thus, to generate two extremas, we need four DoG images. To generate these four DoG images, we need five Gaussian blurred images. Thus, we need five images in a single octave. It has also been found that the optimal results are obtained when $\sigma = 1.6$ and $k = \sqrt{2}$.

The number of keypoints located so far is quite high. Some of these keypoints either lie on an edge or don't have enough contrast to be useful to us. So we need to get rid of these keypoints. This approach is similar to that used in the **Harris corner detector** to remove edges.

To remove low contrast keypoints, we simply compare the intensity value of the current pixel to a preselected threshold value. If it is less than the threshold value, it is rejected. Because we have used subpixel keypoints, we again need to use the Taylor series expansion to get the intensity value at subpixel locations.

For stability, it is not sufficient to reject keypoints with low contrast. The DoG function will have a strong response along edges, even if the location along the edge is poorly determined and therefore, unstable to small amounts of noise.

To eliminate keypoints along the edges, we calculate two gradients at the keypoint, which are perpendicular to each other. The region around the keypoint can be one of the following three types:

- A flat region (both gradients will be small)
- An edge (here, the gradient parallel to the edge will be small, but the one perpendicular to it will be large)
- A corner (both gradients will be large)

As we want only corners as our keypoints, we only accept those keypoints whose both gradient values are high.

To calculate this, we use the **Hessian matrix**. This is similar to the Harris corner detector. In the Harris corner detector, we calculate two different eigenvalues, whereas, in SIFT, we save the computation by just calculating their ratios directly. The Hessian matrix is shown as follows:

$$H = \begin{bmatrix} D_{xx} & D_{xy} \\ D_{xy} & D_{yy} \end{bmatrix}$$

Orientation assignment

Till now, we have stable keypoints and we know the scales at which these were detected. So, we have scale invariance. Now we try to assign an orientation to each keypoint. This orientation helps us achieve rotation invariance.

We try to compute the magnitude and direction of the Gaussian blurred images for each keypoint. The magnitudes and directions are calculated using these formulae:

$$m(x, y) = \sqrt{\left(L(x+1, y) - L(x-1, y)\right)^2 + \left(L(x, y+1) - L(x, y-1)\right)^2}$$

$$\theta(x, y) = \tan^{-1}\left(\left(L(x, y+1) - L(x, y-1)\right) / \left(L(x+1, y) - L(x-1, y)\right)\right)$$

The magnitude and orientation are calculated for all pixels around the keypoint. We create a 36-bin histogram covering the 360-degree range of orientations. Each sample added to the histogram is weighted by its gradient magnitude and by a Gaussian-weighted circular window with σ, which is 1.5 times that of the scale of the keypoint. Suppose you get a histogram, as shown in the following figure:

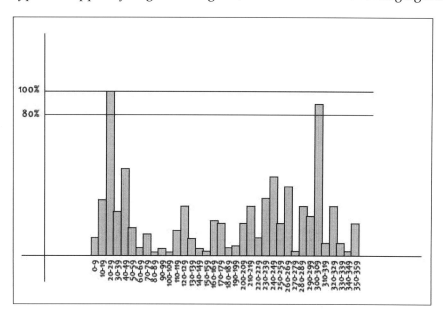

After this has been done for all the neighboring pixels of a particular keypoint, we will get a peak in the histogram. In the preceding figure, we can see that the histogram peaks in the region **20-29**. So, we assign this orientation to the keypoint. Also, any peaks above **80%** value are also converted into keypoints. These new keypoints have the same location and scale as the original keypoint, but its orientation is assigned to the value corresponding to the new peak.

Keypoint descriptor

Till now, we have achieved scale and rotation invariance. We now need to create a descriptor for various keypoints so as to be able to differentiate it from the other keypoints.

To generate a descriptor, we take a 16x16 window around the keypoint and break it into 16 windows of size 4x4. This can be seen in the following image:

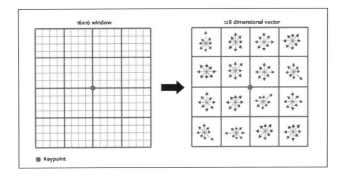

We do this in order to incorporate the fact that objects in two images are rarely never exactly the same. Hence, we try to lose some precision in our calculations. Within each 4x4 window, gradient magnitudes and orientations are calculated. These orientations are put in an 8-bin histogram. Each bin represents an orientation angle of 45 degrees.

Now that we have a large area to consider, we need to take the distance of the vectors from the keypoint into consideration. To achieve this, we use the Gaussian weighting function:

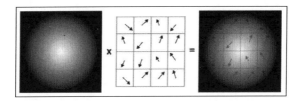

We put the 16 vectors into 8-bin histograms each, and doing this for each of the 4x4 windows we get 4x4x8 = 128 numbers. Once we have all these 128 numbers, we normalize the numbers (by dividing each by the sum of their squares). This set of 128 normalized numbers forms the feature vector.

By the introduction of the feature vector, some unwanted dependencies arise, which are as follows:

- **Rotation dependence**: The feature vector uses gradient orientations. So, if we rotate the image, our feature vector changes and the gradient orientations are also affected. To achieve rotation independence, we subtract the keypoint's rotation from each orientation. Thus, each gradient orientation is now relative to the keypoint's orientation.

- **Illumination dependence**: Illumination independence can be achieved by thresholding large values in the feature vector. So any value greater than 0.2 is changed to 0.2 and the resultant feature vector is normalized again. We have now obtained an illumination independent feature vector.

So, now that we have seen how SIFT works in theory, let's see how it works in OpenCV and its capability to match objects.

 Images and a simplified explanation of SIFT by Utkarsh Sinha can be found at http://www.aishack.in/.

SIFT in OpenCV

We will set up a new application called Chapter3, which is similar to the one created in the earlier chapters. We will make changes to MainActivity.java. Some changes also have to be made to HomeActivity.java, but they will be self-explanatory.

First, we open res | main_menu.xml. In this file, we will create two items. One to select each image to be matched. As a convention, we will have the first image as the object to detect and the second image as the scene in which we want to detect it:

```
<menu xmlns:android="http://schemas.android.com/apk/res/android"
    xmlns:tools="http://schemas.android.com/tools"
    tools:context="com.packtpub.masteringopencvandroid.
      chapter3.MainActivity">
    <item android:id="@+id/action_load_first_image"
        android:title="@string/action_load_first_image"
        android:orderInCategory="1"
        android:showAsAction="never" />
    <item android:id="@+id/action_load_second_image"
        android:title="@string/action_load_second_image"
        android:orderInCategory="2"
        android:showAsAction="never" />
</menu>
```

Now we need to program these items in to our Java code. This is similar to *Chapter 1, Applying Effects to Images*, where we opened the photo picker using intents. We will have two flag variables that will store each image that has been selected. If it is selected, we will perform our computations.

We will perform our actual computations in `AsyncTask`, as these tasks are computationally expensive; and to avoid blocking the UI thread for a long time, we offload the computation onto an asynchronous background worker—AsyncTasks that enables us to perform threading:

```
new AsyncTask<Void, Void, Bitmap>() {
    private long startTime, endTime;
    @Override
    protected void onPreExecute() {
        super.onPreExecute();
        startTime = System.currentTimeMillis();
    }

    @Override
    protected Bitmap doInBackground(Void... params) {
        return executeTask();
    }

    @Override
    protected void onPostExecute(Bitmap bitmap) {
        super.onPostExecute(bitmap);
        endTime = System.currentTimeMillis();
        ivImage1.setImageBitmap(bitmap);
        tvKeyPointsObject1.setText("Object 1 :
          "+keypointsObject1);
        tvKeyPointsObject2.setText("Object 2 :
          "+keypointsObject2);
        tvKeyPointsMatches.setText("Keypoint Matches :
          "+keypointMatches);
        tvTime.setText("Time taken : "+(endTime-startTime)+" ms");
    }
}.execute();
```

Here, the `executeTask` function has been called, which will perform all our computations. First, we need to detect the keypoints, and then we need to use descriptors to describe them.

We first declare all our variables:

```
FeatureDetector detector;
MatOfKeyPoint keypoints1, keypoints2;
DescriptorExtractor descriptorExtractor;
Mat descriptors1, descriptors2;
```

Then, depending on the algorithm, we initialize these variables. For SIFT, we use the following code snippet:

```
switch (ACTION_MODE){
        case HomeActivity.MODE_SIFT:
                detector = FeatureDetector.
                  create(FeatureDetector.SIFT);
                descriptorExtractor = DescriptorExtractor.
                  create(DescriptorExtractor.SIFT);
                //Add SIFT specific code
                break;
        //Add cases for other algorithms
}
```

Now we detect the keypoints:

```
detector.detect(src2, keypoints2);
detector.detect(src1, keypoints1);
keypointsObject1 = keypoints1.toArray().length; //These
  have been added to display the number of keypoints later.
keypointsObject2 = keypoints2.toArray().length;
```

Now that we have the keypoints, we will compute their descriptors:

```
descriptorExtractor.compute(src1, keypoints1, descriptors1);
descriptorExtractor.compute(src2, keypoints2, descriptors2);
```

Matching features and detecting objects

Once we have detected features in two or more objects, and have their descriptors, we can match the features to check whether the images have any similarities. For example, suppose we want to search for a particular book in a heap of many books. OpenCV provides us with two feature matching algorithms:

- Brute-force matcher
- FLANN based matcher

We will see how the two work in the following sections.

For matching, we first need to declare some variables:

```
DescriptorMatcher descriptorMatcher;
MatOfDMatch matches = new MatOfDMatch();
```

Brute-force matcher

It takes the descriptor of one feature in the first set and matches it with all other features in the second set, using distance calculations, and the closest one is returned.

The BF matcher takes two optional parameters. The first one is the distance measurement type, normType. We should use NORM_L2 for descriptors such as SIFT and SURF. For descriptors that are based on a binary string, such as ORB and BRISK, we use NORM_HAMMING as the distance measurement. The second one is crosscheck. If it is set to true, the matcher only returns matches with values (i, j) such that the ith descriptor in the first image has the jth descriptor in the second set, as the best matches, and vice versa.

In our case for SIFT, we add the following code:

```
descriptorMatcher = DescriptorMatcher.create(DescriptorMatcher.
BRUTEFORCE_SL2);
```

FLANN based matcher

FLANN stands for **Fast Library for Approximate Nearest Neighbors**. It contains a collection of algorithms optimized for a fast nearest neighbor search in large datasets and for high-dimensional features. It works faster than the BF matcher for large datasets.

For FLANN based matcher, we need to pass two dictionaries, which specifies the algorithm to be used, its related parameters, and so on. The first one is IndexParams. For various algorithms, the information to be passed is explained in the FLANN docs.

The second dictionary is SearchParams. It specifies the number of times the trees in the index should be recursively traversed. Higher values give better precision, but also take more time.

To use the FLANN based matcher, we need to initialize it as follows:

```
descriptorMatcher =
   DescriptorMatcher.create(DescriptorMatcher.FLANNBASED);
```

Matching the points

Once we have the DescriptorMatcher object, we use the match() and knnMatch() functions. The first one returns all the matches, while the second one returns *k* matches, where *k* is defined by the user.

After we have computed the descriptors, we can use the following to match the keypoints:

```
descriptorMatcher.match(descriptors1, descriptors2, matches);1
```

Now we show the matches obtained using `drawMatches()`, which helps us draw the matches. It stacks two images horizontally and draws lines from the first image to the second image, showing the best matches. There is also a `drawMatchesKnn()` function, which draws all the *k* best matches. If *k = 2*, it will draw two match lines for each keypoint. So, we have to pass a mask if we want to selectively draw it.

To draw the matches, we will add a function that will merge the query and train image into one and also display the matches in the same image:

```
static Mat drawMatches(Mat img1, MatOfKeyPoint key1, Mat img2,
   MatOfKeyPoint key2, MatOfDMatch matches, boolean imageOnly){
        Mat out = new Mat();
        Mat im1 = new Mat();
        Mat im2 = new Mat();
        Imgproc.cvtColor(img1, im1, Imgproc.COLOR_BGR2RGB);
        Imgproc.cvtColor(img2, im2, Imgproc.COLOR_BGR2RGB);
        if (imageOnly){
            MatOfDMatch emptyMatch = new MatOfDMatch();
            MatOfKeyPoint emptyKey1 = new MatOfKeyPoint();
            MatOfKeyPoint emptyKey2 = new MatOfKeyPoint();
            Features2d.drawMatches(im1, emptyKey1,
               im2, emptyKey2, emptyMatch, out);
        } else {
            Features2d.drawMatches(im1, key1,
               im2, key2, matches, out);
        }
        Bitmap bmp = Bitmap.createBitmap(out.cols(),
           out.rows(), Bitmap.Config.ARGB_8888);
        Imgproc.cvtColor(out, out, Imgproc.COLOR_BGR2RGB);
        Core.putText(out, "FRAME", new Point(img1.width() / 2,30),
           Core.FONT_HERSHEY_PLAIN, 2, new Scalar(0,255,255),3);
        Core.putText(out, "MATCHED", new Point(img1.width() +
           img2.width() / 2,30), Core.FONT_HERSHEY_PLAIN, 2, new
           Scalar(255,0,0),3);
        return out;
    }
```

Because SIFT and SURF are patented algorithms, they are not automatically built by OpenCV. We need to manually build the `nonfree` module so as to be able to use them in OpenCV. For this, you will need to download Android NDK, which allows us to use the native C++ code along with the Java code. It is available at `https://developer.android.com/tools/sdk/ndk/index.html`. Then, extract it to a suitable location.

First, you need to download some files from OpenCV's source repository, which is located at `https://github.com/Itseez/opencv/modules/src/`. These are `nonfree_init.cpp`, `precomp.cpp`, `sift.cpp`, and `surf.cpp`. These will also be available with the code for this chapter, so you can download them directly from there as well. Now, create a folder in your `src` directory called `jni` and copy these files to there. We need to modify these files a bit.

Open `precomp.hpp` and remove the lines `#include "cvconfig.h"` and `#include "opencv2/ocl/private/util.hpp"`.

Open `nonfree_init.cpp` and remove the lines of code starting from `#ifdef HAVE_OPENCV_OCL` and ending at `#endif`.

Now we will create a file called `Android.mk` and copy the following lines of code to it. You need to replace `<OpenCV4Android_SDK_location>` accordingly:

```
LOCAL_PATH := $(call my-dir)

include $(CLEAR_VARS)

OPENCV_CAMERA_MODULES:=on
OPENCV_INSTALL_MODULES:=on

include <OpenCV4Android_SDK_location>/sdk/native/jni/OpenCV.mk

LOCAL_MODULE    := nonfree
LOCAL_SRC_FILES := nonfree_init.cpp \
sift.cpp \
surf.cpp
LOCAL_LDLIBS += -llog -ldl
include $(BUILD_SHARED_LIBRARY)
```

Next, create a file named `Application.mk` and copy the following lines of code to it. These define the architecture for which our library would be built:

```
APP_STL := gnustl_static
APP_CPPFLAGS := -frtti -fexceptions
APP_ABI := armeabi-v7a
APP_PLATFORM := android-8
```

Open the `build.gradle` file in your `app` folder. Under the `android` section, add the following:

```
sourceSets.main {
    jniLibs.srcDir 'src/main/libs'
    jni.srcDirs = [] //disable automatic ndk-build call
}
```

Open a terminal or a command window if you are on Windows. Then, change the directory to your project using the `cd` command. Type the following in the command window:

cd <project_directory>/app/src/main/jni

In the terminal window, type the following, replacing <ndk_dir> with the appropriate directory location:

<ndk_dir>/ndk-build

After this, our library should have been successfully built and should be available in the `src` | `obj` folder, under the correct architecture.

Now we need to load this library from our Java code. Open `MainActivity.java`, and in our OpenCV Manager's callback variable (the `mOpenCVCallback` file's `onManagerConnected` function) within the case for `LoaderCallbackInterface.SUCCESS`, add the following line of code:

```
System.loadLibrary("nonfree");
```

The name of the library, nonfree, is the same as the module name defined in the Android.mk file.

SIFT feature matching

Detecting objects

In the previous sections, we detected features in multiple images and matched them to their corresponding features in the other images. The information we obtained is enough to locate objects in a scene.

We use a function from OpenCV's calib3d module, findHomography().Using this function, we can find a perspective transformation of the object, that is, a rotated and skewed result. Then we use perspectiveTransform() to locate the object in the scene. We need at least four matching points to calculate the transformation successfully.

We have seen that there can be some possible errors while matching, which may affect the result. To solve this problem, the algorithm uses either RANSAC or LEAST_MEDIAN (which can be specified by the flags). Good matches that provide the correct estimation are called inliers and the remaining are called outliers. findHomography() returns a mask, which specifies the inlier and outlier points.

Now we will look at the algorithm to implement it.

First, we detect and match keypoints in both the images. This has already been done in the previous sections. Then we set a condition that there has to be a certain number of matches to detect an object.

If enough matches are found, we extract the locations of matched keypoints in both the images. They are passed to find the perspective transformation. Once we get this 3x3 transformation matrix, we use it to transform the corners of `queryImage` to the corresponding points in `trainImage`. Then, we draw it.

Finally, we draw our inliers (if we successfully find the object) or matching keypoints (if it failed).

Speeded Up Robust Features

Speeded Up Robust Features (SURF) was proposed by Herbert Bay, Tinne Tuytelaars, and Luc Van Gool in 2006. Some of the drawbacks of SIFT are that it is slow and computationally expensive. To target this problem, SURF was thought of. Apart from the increase in speed, the other motivations behind SURF were as follows:

- Fast interest point detection

- Distinctive interest point description

- Speeded up descriptor matching

- Invariant to the following common image transformations:

    ○   Image rotation

    ○   Scale changes

    ○   Illumination changes

    ○   Small changes in viewpoint

SURF detector

Just as SIFT approximate Laplacian of Gaussian images to Difference of Gaussian, SURF uses integral images to approximate Laplacian of Gaussian images. An integral image (summed area tables) is an intermediate representation of the image and contains the sum of grayscale pixel values of the image. It is called the **fast Hessian** detector. The descriptor, on the other hand, describes a distribution of Haar wavelet responses within the interest point neighborhood.

You can refer to the paper at `http://www.vision.ee.ethz.ch/~surf/eccv06.pdf`.

To select the location and scale of keypoints, SURF uses the determinant of the Hessian matrix. SURF proves that Gaussian is overrated as the property that no new structures can appear while going down to lower resolutions has only been proved in 1D, but does not apply to the 2D case. Given SIFT's success with the LoG approximation, SURF further approximates LoG using box filters. Box filters approximate Gaussians and can be calculated very quickly. The following image shows an approximation of Gaussians as box filters:

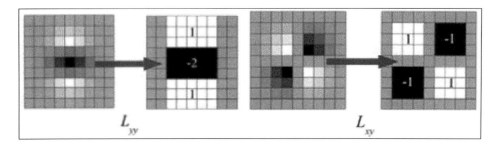

Due to the use of box filters and integral images, we no longer have to perform repeated Gaussian smoothing. We apply box filters of different sizes directly to the integral image. Instead of iteratively down-scaling images, we up-scale the filter size. Hence, scale analysis is done using only a single image. The output of the preceding 9x9 filter is considered as the initial scale layer. Other layers are obtained by filtering, using gradually bigger filters. Images of the first octave are obtained using filters of size 9x9, 15x15, 21x21, and 27x27. At larger scales, the step size between the filters should also scale accordingly. Hence, for each new octave, the filter size step is doubled (that is, from 6 to 12 to 24). In the next octave, the filter sizes are 39x39, 51x51, and so on.

In order to localize interest points in the image and over scales, a non-maximum suppression in a 3x3x3 neighborhood is applied. The maxima of the determinant of the Hessian matrix is then interpolated in scale and image space using the method proposed by Brown, and others. Scale space interpolation is especially important in our case, as the difference in scale between the first layers of every octave is relatively large.

SURF descriptor

Now that we have localized the keypoints, we need to create a descriptor for each, so as to uniquely identify it from other keypoints. SURF works on similar principles of SIFT, but with lesser complexity. Bay and others also proposed a variation of SURF that doesn't take rotation invariance into account, which is called **U-SURF** (upright SURF). In many applications, the camera orientation remains more or less constant. Hence, we can save a lot of computation by ignoring rotation invariance.

First, we need to fix a reproducible orientation based on the information obtained from a circular region centered about the keypoint. Then we construct a square region that is rotated and aligned based on the selected orientation, and then we can extract the SURF descriptor from it.

Orientation assignment

In order to add rotation invariance, the orientation of the keypoints must be robust and reproducible. For this, SURF proposes calculating Haar wavelet responses in the x and y directions. The responses are calculated in a circular neighborhood of radius 6 s around the keypoint, where s is the scale of the image (that is, the value of σ). To calculate the Haar wavelet responses, SURF proposes using a wavelet size of 4 s. After obtaining the wavelet responses and weighing them with a Gaussian kernel $(\sigma = 2.5s)$ centered about the keypoint, the responses are represented as vectors. The vectors are represented as the response strength in the horizontal direction along the abscissa, and the response strength in the vertical direction along the ordinate. All the responses within a sliding orientation window covering an angle of 60 degrees are then summed up. The longest vector calculated is set as the direction of the descriptor:

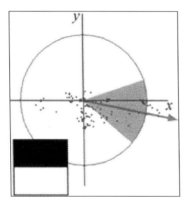

Haar wavelet responses in a 60 degree angle

The size of the sliding window is taken as a parameter, which has to be calculated experimentally. Small window sizes result in single dominating wavelet responses, whereas large window sizes result in maxima in vector lengths that are not descriptive enough. Both result in an unstable orientation of the interest region. This step is skipped for U-SURF, as it is doesn't require rotation invariance.

Descriptor based on Haar wavelet responses

For the extraction of the descriptor, the first step consists of constructing a square region centered around the interest point and oriented along the orientation selected in the previous section. This is not required for U-SURF. The size of the window is 20 s. The steps to find the descriptor are as follows:

1. Split the interest region into 4x4 square subregions with 5x5 regularly spaced sample points inside.

2. Calculate Haar wavelet responses d^x and d^y [d^x = Haar wavelet response in x direction; d^y = Haar wavelet response in y direction. The filter size used is 2 s].

3. Weight the response with a Gaussian kernel centered at the interest point.

4. Sum the response over each subregion for d^x and d^y separately, to form a feature vector of length 32.

5. In order to bring in information about the polarity of the intensity changes, extract the sum of the absolute value of the responses, which is a feature vector of length 64.

6. Normalize the vector to unit length.

The wavelet responses are invariant to a bias in illumination (offset). Invariance to contrast (a scale factor) is achieved by turning the descriptor into a unit vector (normalization).

Experimentally, Bay and others tested a variation of SURF that adds some more features (SURF-128). The sums of d^x and $|d^x|$ are computed separately for $d^y < 0$ and $d^y \geq 0$. Similarly, the sums of d^y and $|d^y|$ are split according to the sign of d^x, thereby doubling the number of features. This version of SURF-128 outperforms SURF.

The following table shows a comparison between the various algorithms in finding features:

	U-SURF	SURF	SIFT
Time (ms)	225	354	1036

While SIFT and SURF work well in finding good features, they are **patented** for commercial use. So, you have to pay some money if you use them for commercial purposes.

Some of the results we obtain from SURF are as follows:

- SURF is faster than SIFT by three times and has a recall precision no worse than SIFT
- SURF is good at handling images with blurring or rotation
- SURF is poor at handling images with viewpoint changes

SURF in OpenCV

The code for SURF needs only a little modification. We just need to add a case in our switch case construct:

```
case HomeActivity.MODE_SURF:
    detector = FeatureDetector.create(FeatureDetector.SURF);
    descriptorExtractor = DescriptorExtractor.
      create(DescriptorExtractor.SURF);
    descriptorMatcher = DescriptorMatcher.
      create(DescriptorMatcher.BRUTEFORCE_SL2);
    break;
```

SURF feature matching

Oriented FAST and Rotated BRIEF

Oriented FAST and Rotated BRIEF (ORB) was developed at OpenCV labs by Ethan Rublee, Vincent Rabaud, Kurt Konolige, and Gary R. Bradski in 2011, as an efficient and viable alternative to SIFT and SURF. ORB was conceived mainly because SIFT and SURF are patented algorithms. ORB, however, is free to use.

ORB performs as well as SIFT on these tasks (and better than SURF), while being almost two order of magnitude faster. ORB builds on the well-known FAST keypoint detector and the BRIEF descriptor. Both these techniques are attractive because of their good performance and low cost. ORB's main contributions are as follows:

- The addition of a fast and accurate orientation component to FAST
- The efficient computation of oriented BRIEF features
- Analysis of variance and correlation of oriented BRIEF features
- A learning method for decorrelating BRIEF features under rotational invariance, leading to better performance in nearest-neighbor applications

oFAST – FAST keypoint orientation

FAST is a feature detection algorithm that is widely recognized due its fast computation properties. It doesn't propose a descriptor to uniquely identify features. Moreover, it does not have any orientation component, so it performs poorly to in-plane rotation and scale changes. We will take a look at how ORB added an orientation component to FAST features.

FAST detector

First, we detect FAST keypoints. FAST takes one parameter from the user, the threshold value between the center pixel, and those in a circular ring around it. We use a ring radius of 9 pixels as it gives good performance. FAST also produces keypoints that are along edges. To overcome this, we use the Harris corner measure to order the keypoints. If we want N keypoints, we first keep the threshold low enough to generate more than N keypoints, and then pick the topmost N based on the Harris corner measure.

FAST does not produce multiscale features. ORB employs a scale pyramid of the image and produces FAST features (filtered by Harris) at each level in the pyramid.

Orientation by intensity centroid

To assign orientation to corners, we use the intensity centroid. We assume that the corner is offset from the intensity centroid and this vector is used to assign orientation to a keypoint.

To compute the coordinates of the centroid, we use moments. Moments are calculated as follows:

$$m_{pq} = \sum_{x,y} x^p y^q I(x, y)$$

The coordinates of the centroid can be calculated as follows:

$$C = \left(\frac{m_{10}}{m_{00}}, \frac{m_{01}}{m_{00}} \right)$$

We construct a vector $\overrightarrow{OC}$ from the keypoint's center, O, to the centroid, C. The orientation of the patch is obtained by:

$$\theta = atan2\left(m_{01}, m_{10}\right)$$

Here, *atan2* is the quadrant-aware version of *arctan*. To improve the rotation invariance of this measure, we make sure that the moments are computed with x and y remaining within a circular region of radius r. We empirically choose r to be the patch size so that x and y run from $[-r, r]$. As $|C|$ approaches 0, the measure becomes unstable; with FAST corners, we have found that this is rarely the case. This method can also work well in images with heavy noise.

rBRIEF – Rotation-aware BRIEF

BRIEF is a feature description algorithm that is also known for its fast speed of computation. However, BRIEF also isn't invariant to rotation. ORB tries to add this functionality, without losing out on the speed aspect of BRIEF. The feature vector obtained by n binary tests in BRIEF is as follows:

$$f(n) = \sum_{1 < i < n} 2^{i-1} \tau\left(p; x_i, y_i\right)$$

Where $\tau(p;x,y)$ is defined as:

$$\tau(p;x,y) = \begin{cases} 1 & : p(x) < p(y) \\ 0 & : p(x) \geq p(y) \end{cases}$$

p(x) is the intensity value at pixel *x*.

Steered BRIEF

The matching performance of BRIEF falls off sharply for in-plane rotation of more than a few degrees. ORB proposes a method to steer BRIEF according to the orientation of the keypoints. For any feature set of n binary tests at location (xⁱ, yⁱ), we define the *2 x n* matrix:

$$S = \begin{pmatrix} x1,\ldots,xn \\ y1,\ldots,yn \end{pmatrix}$$

We use the patch orientation θ and the corresponding rotation matrix R^θ, and construct a *steered* version S^θ of S:

$$S_\theta = R_\theta S$$

Now the steered BRIEF operator becomes:

$$g_n(p,\theta) = f_n(p) | (x_i,y_i) \in S_\theta$$

We discretize the angle to increments of $2\pi/30$ (12 degrees), and construct a lookup table of precomputed BRIEF patterns. As long as the keypoint orientation θ is consistent across views, the correct set of points S^θ will be used to compute its descriptor.

Variance and correlation

One of the properties of BRIEF is that each bit feature has a large variance and a mean near 0.5. A mean of 0.5 gives a maximum sample variance of 0.25 for a bit feature. Steered BRIEF produces a more uniform appearance to binary tests. High variance causes a feature to respond more differently to inputs.

Having uncorrelated features is desirable as in that case, each test has a contribution to the results. We search among all the possible binary tests to find ones that have a high variance (and a mean close to 0.5) as well as being uncorrelated.

ORB specifies the rBRIEF algorithm as follows:

Set up a training set of some 300 k keypoints drawn from images in the PASCAL 2006 set. Then, enumerate all the possible binary tests drawn from a 31x31 pixel patch. Each test is a pair of 5x5 subwindows of the patch. If we note the width of our patch as $w^p = 31$ and the width of the test subwindow as $w^t = 5$, then we have $N = (wp - w^t)^2$ possible subwindows. We would like to select pairs of two from these, so we have $\binom{N}{2}$ 2 binary tests. We eliminate tests that overlap, so we end up with $N = 205590$ possible tests. The algorithm is as follows:

- Run each test against all training patches.

- Order the tests by their distance from a mean of 0.5, forming the vector T.

- Perform a greedy search:

  ○ Put the first test into the result vector R and remove it from T.

  ○ Take the next test from T, and compare it against all tests in R. If its absolute correlation is greater than a threshold, discard it; else add it to R.

  ○ Repeat the previous step until there are 256 tests in R. If there are fewer than 256, raise the threshold and try again.

rBRIEF shows significant improvement in the variance and correlation over steered BRIEF. ORB outperforms SIFT and SURF on the outdoor dataset. It is about the same on the indoor set; note that blob detection keypoints, such as SIFT, tend to be better on graffiti type images.

ORB in OpenCV

The code for ORB is similar to SIFT and SURF. However, ORB being a binary string-based descriptor, we will use the hamming code in our BF matcher.

The code for SURF needs only a little modification. We just need to add a case to our switch case construct:

```
case HomeActivity.MODE_ORB:
    detector = FeatureDetector.create(FeatureDetector.ORB);
    descriptorExtractor = DescriptorExtractor.
      create(DescriptorExtractor.ORB);
```

```
descriptorMatcher = DescriptorMatcher.
  create(DescriptorMatcher.BRUTEFORCE_HAMMING);
break;
```

ORB feature matching

Binary Robust Invariant Scalable Keypoints

Binary Robust Invariant Scalable Keypoints (BRISK) was conceived by Leutenegger, Chli, and Siegwart to be an efficient replacement to the state-of-the-art feature detection, description, and matching algorithms. The motivation behind BRISK was to develop a robust algorithm that can reproduce features in a computationally efficient manner. In some cases, BRISK achieves comparable quality of feature matching as SURF, while requiring much less computation time.

Scale-space keypoint detection

The BRISK detector is based on the AGAST detector, which is an extension of a faster performance version of FAST. To achieve scale invariance, BRISK searches for the maxima in a scale space using the FAST score(s) as the comparison parameter. Despite discretizing the scale axis at coarser intervals than in alternative high-performance detectors (for example, the fast Hessian), the BRISK detector estimates the true scale of each keypoint in the continuous scale space. The BRISK scale space comprises of n octaves, c^i and n intra-octaves, and d^i $[i = \{0, 1, 2, ..., n-1\}]$. BRISK suggests using $n = 4$.

The original image is taken as c^0, and each successive octave is half-sampled from the previous octave. Each intra-octave d^i is down-sampled such that it lies between c^i and c^i+1. The first intra-octave d^0 is obtained by down sampling c^0 by a factor of 1.5. The subsequent intra-octaves are obtained by half sampling the previous intra-octave.

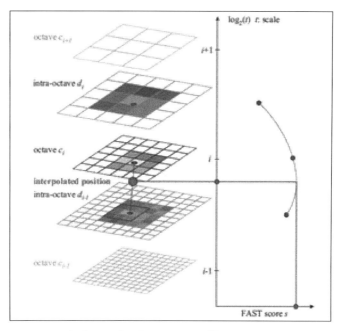

An image showing octaves and intra-octaves

The FAST 9-16 detector requires that in a 16 pixel circular radius, at least 9 pixels must be brighter than or darker than the center pixel for the FAST criterion to be fulfilled. BRISK proposes the use of this FAST 9-16 detector.

The FAST score is computed for each octave and intra-octave separately. The FAST detector score, s, is calculated for each pixel as the maximum threshold for FAST detection, such that an image point is considered as a corner.

A non-maximum suppression in scale space is carried out on the keypoints obtained after applying the FAST 9-16 detector. The keypoint should be the maximum among its eight neighboring FAST scores in the same octave or intra-octave. This point must also have a higher FAST score than points in the layers above and below it. We then check inside the equally sized square patches having a 2 pixel side length in the layer, where the maximum value is suspected to be present. Interpolation is carried out at the boundaries of the patch, as neighboring layers are represented with different discretizations than that of the current later.

We try to calculate a subpixel location for each maximum detected in the earlier step. A 2D quadratic function is fitted to the 3x3 patch surrounding the pixel, and the subpixel maximum is determined. This is also done for the layers above and below the current layer. These maximas are then interpolated using a 1D parabola across the scale space, and the local maximum is chosen as the scale for the feature is found.

Keypoint description

The BRISK descriptor is composed of a binary string by concatenating the results of simple brightness comparison tests. In BRISK, we need to identify the characteristic direction of each keypoint to achieve the rotation invariance.

Sampling pattern and rotation estimation

The BRISK descriptor makes use of a pattern used for sampling the neighborhood of the keypoint. The pattern defines N locations equally spaced on circles concentric with the keypoint, as shown in the following figure:

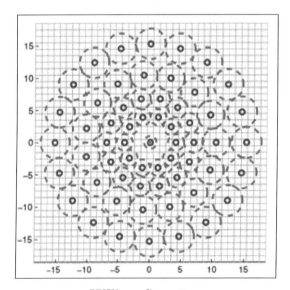

BRISK sampling pattern

In order to avoid aliasing effects when sampling the image intensity of a point p^i in the pattern, we apply Gaussian smoothing with the standard deviation σ_i proportional to the distance between the points on the respective circles. We then calculate the gradient between two sampling points.

The formula used is:

$$g(p_i, p_j) = (p_j - p_i) \frac{I(p_j, \sigma_j) - I(p_i, \sigma_i)}{\|p_j - p_i\|^2} \|p_j - p_i\|^2$$

BRISK defines a subset of short distance pairings, S, and another subset of long distance pairings, L, as follows:

$$S = \left\{ (p_i, p_j) \in A \mid \|p_j - p_i\| < \delta_{max} \right\}$$

$$L = \left\{ (p_i, p_j) \in A \mid \|p_j - p_i\| > \delta_{max} \right\}$$

Where A is the set of all sampling point pairs as follows:

$$A = \left\{ (p_i, p_j) \in \mathbb{R}^2 * \mathbb{R}^2 \mid i < N^j < i^i, j \in \mathbb{N} \right\}$$

The threshold distances are set to $\delta_{max} = 9.75t$ and $\delta_{min} = 13.67t$ (t is the scale of the keypoint). BRISK estimates the overall characteristic pattern direction of the keypoint k to be:

$$g = \begin{pmatrix} g_x \\ g_y \end{pmatrix} = \frac{1}{|L|} \sum_{(pi, pj) \in L} g(p_i, p_j)$$

Building the descriptor

In order to develop a rotation and scale invariant descriptor, BRISK applies the sampling pattern rotated by an angle, $\alpha = arctan2(g_y, g_x)$, around the keypoint k. Short distance intensity comparisons of point pairs, $(p_i^\alpha, p_j^\alpha) \in S$ (that is, in the rotated pattern), are calculated to get the bit vector descriptor d^k. Each bit b corresponds to:

$$b = \begin{cases} 1, & I(p_j^\alpha, \sigma_j) > I(p_i^\alpha, \sigma_i) \\ 0, & Otherwise \end{cases}$$

$$\forall (p_i^\alpha, p_j^\alpha) \in S$$

BRISK uses a deterministic sampling pattern, resulting in a uniform sampling point density at a given radius around the keypoint. Due to this, the Gaussian smoothing does not modify the information content of a brightness comparison by blurring two close sampling points while comparing them. BRISK uses a lesser number of sampling points than a simple pairwise comparison (because a single point participates in more comparisons), thereby reducing the complexity of looking up the intensity values. As the brightness variations only need to be locally consistent, the comparisons done here are restricted spatially. We obtain a bit string of length 512 using the sampling pattern and the distance thresholds as shown previously.

BRISK In OpenCV

Again, the only change that we will make is to add another case to our switch case construct:

```
case HomeActivity.MODE_BRISK:
    detector = FeatureDetector.create(FeatureDetector.BRISK);
    descriptorExtractor = DescriptorExtractor.
      create(DescriptorExtractor.BRISK);
    descriptorMatcher = DescriptorMatcher.
      create(DescriptorMatcher.BRUTEFORCE_HAMMING);
    break;
```

BRISK feature matching

Fast Retina Keypoint

Fast Retina Keypoint (FREAK) proposes a robust descriptor to uniquely identify keypoints and in the process, require less computation time and memory. FREAK has been inspired by the human retina.

A retinal sampling pattern

FREAK proposes to use the retinal sampling grid, which is also circular, with the difference of having higher density of points near the center. The density of points drops exponentially as we move away from the center point. This is similar to BRISK, except for the exponential decrease.

Each keypoint needs to be smoothed to be less sensitive to noise. Unlike BRIEF and ORB, which use the same kernel for all points, FREAK uses a different kernel for each keypoint. The radius of the Gaussian kernel is proportional to the value of σ.

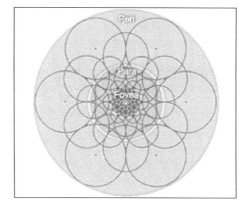

Retinal sampling pattern

FREAK follows ORB's approach and tries to learn about the pairs by maximizing the variance of the pairs and taking pairs that are not correlated, so as to provide maximum information on each keypoint.

A coarse-to-fine descriptor

We need to find pairs of sampling points in order to create a bit-vector. We use a method similar to ORB, that is, instead of matching each pair, we try to learn about which pairs would give the best results. We need to find points that are not correlated. The algorithm is as follows:

- We create a matrix D of nearly 50,000 extracted keypoints. Each row corresponds to a keypoint that is represented with its large descriptor made of all possible pairs in the retina sampling pattern. We use 43 receptive fields, leading to about 1,000 pairs.

- We compute the mean of each column. A mean of 0.5 produces the highest variance.

- Order the columns according to the variance in descending order.

- Select the best column and iteratively add the remaining columns so that they have low correlation with the chosen columns.

In this approach, we first select pairs that compare sampling points in the outer regions, whereas the last pairs are comparison points in the inner rings of the pattern. This is similar to how our retina works in the sense that we first try to locate an object and then try to verify it by precisely matching points that are densely located near the object.

Saccadic search

Humans do not look at a scene in a fixed manner. Their eyes move around with discontinuous individual movements called saccades. The fovea captures high-resolution information; hence, it is critical in the recognition and matching of objects. The perifoveal region captures low-resolution information, and hence, it used to approximately locate objects.

FREAK tries to mimic this function of the retina by searching the first 16 bytes of the descriptor, representing the coarse information. If the distance is smaller than a threshold, we continue by searching the next bytes to obtain a more refined result. Due to this, a cascade of comparisons is performed, accelerating the matching step even further as more than 90 percent of the sampling points are discarded with the first 16 byte comparisons.

Orientation

The method FREAK uses to assign orientation is similar to that of BRISK with the difference being that, instead of using long distance pairs, FREAK uses a predefined set of 45 symmetric sampling pairs.

FREAK in OpenCV

The code for FREAK is similar to that used for the previous algorithms. However, given that FREAK just provides a descriptor, we will use the FAST detector to detect keypoints:

```
case HomeActivity.MODE_FREAK:
    detector = FeatureDetector.create(FeatureDetector.FAST);
    descriptorExtractor = DescriptorExtractor.
      create(DescriptorExtractor.FREAK);
    descriptorMatcher = DescriptorMatcher.
      create(DescriptorMatcher.BRUTEFORCE_HAMMING);
    break;
```

FREAK feature matching

Summary

In this chapter, we have seen how to detect features in an image and match them to features in other images. To perform this task, we looked at various algorithms, such as SIFT, SURF, ORB, BRISK, and FREAK, and their pros and cons. We also saw how we can use these to localize specific objects in a scene. There is one restriction to these methods in that the exact object must be present in the scene image to be detected correctly. In the next chapter, we will take a step forward to detect more general classes of objects, such as human beings, faces, hands, and so on.

4
Drilling Deeper into Object Detection – Using Cascade Classifiers

In the previous chapter, we looked at some very sophisticated algorithms used for object detection. In this chapter, we plan to look further into a different set of algorithms, known as cascade classifiers and HOG descriptors. These algorithms are widely used to detect human expressions and find application in surveillance systems, face recognition systems, and other simple biometric systems. Face detection was one of the first applications of **cascade classifiers** (Haar-cascade classifier) and from then on, there have been many different applications that have been developed.

Have you ever wondered how cameras detect smiling faces in an image and click a picture automatically? It is no rocket science. This chapter will talk about the different ways of detecting human expressions, using which you can build your own version of the aforementioned applications on an Android platform.

We will take a look at the following algorithms in this chapter:

- Cascade classifiers
- HOG descriptors

An introduction to cascade classifiers

What are cascade classifiers? Let's take a look at both the words individually and then combine them to see what the phrase actually means. Classifiers are like black boxes that classify objects into various classes on the basis of a training set. Initially, we take a large set of training data, feed it to any learning algorithm, and compute a trained model (classifier), which is capable of classifying new unknown data.

Let's understand the word cascade. In the literal sense of the word, cascading means to form a chain. In the current context, cascading implies forming a multistage classifier, where the output of one stage is passed on to the next stage, and so on. Cascade classifiers are used in situations where you have low computational power and you do not want to compromise on the speed of your algorithm.

Cascade classifiers that will be covered in this chapter are as follows:

- Haar cascades (Viola and Jones – face detection)
- LBP cascades

Let's briefly understand Haar and LBP Cascades and then build an Android application that uses these cascades to detect faces in images.

Haar cascades

One of the first real-time face detection algorithms, developed by Viola and Jones, was inspired by the concept of Haar wavelets. The algorithm exploits the inherent structure and similarities in human faces. For example, in every human face, the eye region is darker than the cheeks, and the nose bridge region is darker than the eyes. Using such characteristics of a human face, we learn the generic models of the face and then use these trained models to detect faces in images.

Initially, we feed a learning algorithm with positive images (images with faces) and negative images (images with out faces) and learn the classifier. Then we extract Haar features from the images using convolutional kernels (as shown in the following image). Feature values are obtained by subtracting the sum of white pixels under the white rectangle from the sum of pixels under the black rectangle. We slide these kernels (nothing but Haar features) over the entire image and calculate the feature values. If the value is above a certain user-defined threshold, we say that there is a match, otherwise we reject that region. To reduce calculations, we make use of integral images.

An explanation of integral images can be found at
`http://en.wikipedia.org/wiki/Summed_area_table`.

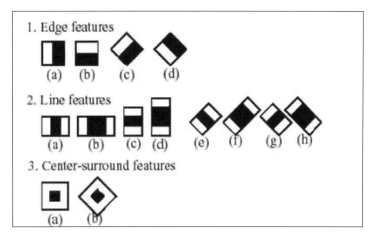

Haar features

Training the classifier every time before using it is unacceptable in terms of the performance because it takes a lot of time; sometimes up to 6-7 hours or more. Hence, we use the pretrained classifiers provided by OpenCV (or any other source).

LBP cascades

The **Local Binary Patterns (LBP)** cascade is another type of a cascade classifier that is used widely in computer vision. Compared to Haar cascades, LBP cascades deal with integers rather than double values. So, both training and testing is faster with LBP cascades and hence is preferred while developing embedded applications. Another important property of LBP is their tolerance against illumination variations.

In LBP, an 8-bit binary feature vector is created for each pixel in the image by considering the eight neighboring pixels (top-left, top-right, left, right, bottom-left, and bottom-right). For every neighboring pixel, there is a corresponding bit which is assigned a value 1 if the pixel value is greater than the center pixel's value, otherwise 0. The 8-bit feature vector is treated as a binary number (later convert it to a decimal value), and using the decimal values for each pixel, a 256-bin histogram is computed. This histogram is used as a representative of the image.

LBP features have some primitives coded in them, as shown in the following image:

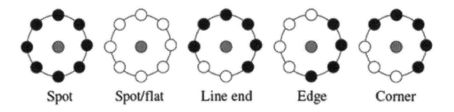

Examples of texture primitives

For Haar cascade, we also make a set of positive images (with faces) and negative images (without faces). We compute histograms for each image and feed it to any learning algorithm.

Face detection using the cascade classifier

One of the most common applications of the cascade classifier is face detection. Implementation for both Haar and LBP classifiers on Android using OpenCV is very similar; the only difference is in the model that we use to detect faces. Let's work on a generic application for face detection and make relevant changes to the application to accommodate both Haar and LBP cascades. The application will display the camera preview on the entire screen (landscape orientation) and make rectangles around faces in each frame. It will also provide an option to switch between the front and back camera. Following are the steps to create this application:

1. Create a new Eclipse (or Android Studio) project with a blank activity and call the application *Face Detection*. It will be a landscape application with a fullscreen camera preview.

2. In the application tag, add the following line to make a fullscreen application:

   ```
   android:theme="@android:style/Theme.NoTitleBar.Fullscreen"
   ```

3. Give the following permissions in `AndroidManifest.xml`:

   ```
   <uses-permission android:name="android.permission.CAMERA"/>
       <uses-feature android:name="android.hardware.camera"
         android:required="false"/>
       <uses-feature android:name="android.hardware.camera.
         autofocus"        android:required="false"/>
   ```

```
<uses-feature android:name="android.hardware.camera.
  front" android:required="false"/>
<uses-feature android:name="android.hardware.camera.
  front.autofocus" android:required="false"/>
```

4. In the main activity, add a camera preview view. This will display the camera's output on the screen. Add the view using the following lines:

```
<org.opencv.android.JavaCameraView
       android:layout_width="fill_parent"
       android:layout_height="fill_parent"
       android:id="@+id/java_surface_view" />
```

OpenCV provides two camera preview views: JavaCameraView and NativeCameraView. Both the views work in a similar way except for a few differences. Refer to http://docs.opencv.org/doc/tutorials/introduction/android_binary_package/dev_with_OCV_on_Android.html?highlight=nativecameraview for a detailed explanation of the differences.

In this application, we will implement the CvCameraViewListener2 interface that has function definitions that provide some control over the camera (refer to the camera preview tutorial of OpenCV). We will take a look at these functions later in this section.

Unlike other applications seen so far in this book, this application has a different implementation of the BaseLoaderCallback class (for those who are not able to recollect, the BaseLoaderCallback class initializes and loads OpenCV modules in the application).

For this application, we will load the cascade classifiers after we have loaded OpenCV in our application. Here is the BaseLoaderCallback class for this application:

```
private BaseLoaderCallback mLoaderCallback = new
  BaseLoaderCallback(this) {
        @Override
        public void onManagerConnected(int status) {
            switch (status) {
                case LoaderCallbackInterface.SUCCESS:
                {
                    Log.i(TAG, "OpenCV loaded successfully");
                    try{
                        InputStream is = getResources().
                          openRawResource(
                          <INSERT_RESOURCE_IDENTIFIER>);
```

```
                            File cascadeDir = getDir("cascade",
                              Context.MODE_PRIVATE);
                            mCascadeFile = new File(cascadeDir,
                              "cascade.xml");
                            FileOutputStream os = new
                              FileOutputStream(mCascadeFile);

                            byte[] buffer = new byte[4096];
                            int bytesRead;
                            while((bytesRead = is.read(buffer)) != -1)
                            {
                                os.write(buffer, 0, bytesRead);
                            }
                            is.close();
                            os.close();

                            haarCascade = new
                              CascadeClassifier(
                              mCascadeFile.getAbsolutePath());
                            if (haarCascade.empty())
                            {
                                Log.i("Cascade Error","Failed to load
                                  cascade classifier");
                                haarCascade = null;
                            }
                        }
                        catch(Exception e)
                        {
                            Log.i("Cascade Error: ","Cascase not
                              found");
                        }
                        mOpenCvCameraView.enableView();
                    } break;
                    default:
                    {
                        super.onManagerConnected(status);
                    } break;
                }
            }
        };
```

In the preceding code snippet, we first check whether OpenCV was successfully loaded. After doing this, we copy the cascade file from the project resources to our application using InputStream and FileOutputStream, as shown next. Create a new folder cascade and copy the contents of the cascade file to a new file in that folder. Now comes the difference between using Haar cascades and LBP cascades. Replace <INSERT_RESOURCE_IDENTIFIER> with your favorite cascade file.

Note: The rest of the code works independently of your choice of the type of cascade.

 OpenCV provides pre-learnt cascades for both Haar and LBP. Copy the cascade file to the `res/raw` folder in your Android project. Let's assume that your cascade files for Haar and LBP are named `haar_cascade.xml` and `lbp_cascade.xml` respectively. Replace `<INSERT_RESOURCE_IDENTIFIER>` with `R.raw.id.haar_casacde` or `R.raw.id.lbp_cascade`, depending on which classifier you want to use.

The reason why we copy and save at the same time is to bring the file from your project directory into your phone's filesystem:

```
InputStream is = getResources().openRawResource
  (<INSERT_RESOURCE_IDENTIFIER>);
File cascadeDir = getDir("cascade", Context.MODE_PRIVATE);
mCascadeFile = new File(cascadeDir, "cascade.xml");
FileOutputStream os = new FileOutputStream(mCascadeFile);

byte[] buffer = new byte[4096];
int bytesRead;
while((bytesRead = is.read(buffer)) != -1)
{
os.write(buffer, 0, bytesRead);
}
is.close();
os.close();
```

After this is done, create a new `CascadeClassifier` object that will be used later to detect faces in the camera feed, as shown in the following code snippet:

```
haarCascade = new CascadeClassifier(mCascadeFile.getAbsolutePath());
if (cascade.empty())
{
    Log.i("Cascade Error","Failed to load cascade classifier");
    cascade = null;
}
```

So far, we have been able to initialize OpenCV in our project, and we have loaded our favorite cascade classifier in to the application. The next step is to get our camera preview ready. As mentioned earlier, we are implementing the `CvCameraViewListener2` interface and hence, we need to implement its member functions:

```
@Override
public void onCameraViewStarted(int width, int height) {
    mRgba = new Mat(height, width, CvType.CV_8UC4);
}

@Override
public void onPause()
{
    super.onPause();
    if (mOpenCvCameraView != null)
        mOpenCvCameraView.disableView();
}

@Override
public void onResume()
{
    super.onResume();
    OpenCVLoader.initAsync(OpenCVLoader.
      OPENCV_VERSION_2_4_9, this, mLoaderCallback);
}

public void onDestroy() {
    super.onDestroy();
    if (mOpenCvCameraView != null)
        mOpenCvCameraView.disableView();
}
```

Another function that needs to be implemented is `onCameraFrame()`. This is where all the magic happens. In this function, we will process each frame and find faces in it:

```
@Override
    public Mat onCameraFrame(CameraBridgeViewBase.
      CvCameraViewFrame inputFrame) {

        //Rotating the input frame
        Mat mGray = inputFrame.gray();
        mRgba = inputFrame.rgba();
```

Chapter 4

```
    if (mIsFrontCamera)
    {
        Core.flip(mRgba, mRgba, 1);
    }


    //Detecting face in the frame
    MatOfRect faces = new MatOfRect();
    if(cascade != null)
    {
        cascade.detectMultiScale(mGray, faces, 1.1, 2,
            2, new Size(200,200), new Size());
    }

    Rect[] facesArray = faces.toArray();
    for (int i = 0; i < facesArray.length; i++)
        Core.rectangle(mRgba, facesArray[i].tl(),
            facesArray[i].br(), new Scalar(100), 3);
    return mRgba;
}
```

Here, we first store the output of the camera in mRgba, and mGray stores the grayscale image of the camera output. Then we check whether we are using the front camera or the back camera of our phone (how to handle the front camera is explained later in this chapter) through a Boolean value mIsFrontCamera (data member of the class). If the front camera is being used, just flip the image. Now create a MatOfRect object that will store the rectangles that bound the faces in the frame. Then, call the magical function:

```
cascade.detectMultiScale(mGray, faces, 1.1, 2,
    2, new Size(200,200), new Size());
```

The detectMultiScale() function takes in a grayscale image and returns rectangles that bound the faces (if any). The third parameter of the function is the scaling factor that specifies how much the image size is reduced at each image scale. For more accurate results, face detection happens at different scales. The last two parameters are the minimum and maximum size of the face that can be detected. These parameters sort of decide the speed at which your application runs. Having a minimum size can make your application perform poorly, that is, have very few frames per second. Be careful while setting these parameters.

Done! The application is almost complete with just one bit of functionality remaining: handling the front camera. In order to do this, follow these steps:

1. We first add a menu option in the application's menu that allows the user to switch between the front and back camera, as follows:

```
@Override
    public boolean onCreateOptionsMenu(Menu menu) {
        // Inflate the menu; this adds items
          to the action bar if it is present.
        getMenuInflater().inflate(R.menu.menu_main, menu);
        Log.i(TAG, "called onCreateOptionsMenu");
        mItemSwitchCamera = menu.add("Toggle
          Front/Back camera");
        return true;
    }
```

2. In the `onOptionsItemSelected()` function, add the functionality to switch between cameras:

```
@Override
    public boolean onOptionsItemSelected(MenuItem item) {
        String toastMesage = "";

        if (item == mItemSwitchCamera) {
            mOpenCvCameraView.setVisibility
              (SurfaceView.GONE);
            mIsFrontCamera = !mIsFrontCamera;
            mOpenCvCameraView = (CameraBridgeViewBase)
              findViewById(R.id.java_surface_view);
            if (mIsFrontCamera) {

                mOpenCvCameraView.setCameraIndex(1);
                toastMesage = "Front Camera";
            } else {
                mOpenCvCameraView.setCameraIndex(-1);
                toastMesage = "Back Camera";
            }

            mOpenCvCameraView.setVisibility
              (SurfaceView.VISIBLE);
            mOpenCvCameraView
              .setCvCameraViewListener(this);
            mOpenCvCameraView.enableView();
```

```
Toast toast = Toast.makeText(this,
    toastMesage, Toast.LENGTH_LONG);
toast.show();
}

return true;
}
```

3. Whenever the user selects this option, we first toggle the `isFrontCamera` value. After this, we change the camera index of the `mOpenCvCameraView` object by running the following code:

```
mOpenCvCameraView.setCameraIndex(-1);
```

The default camera index in Android is `-1`, which represents the back camera. The front camera's index is 1 (this is not a fixed number; it can vary from one phone to another). Set the camera index according to the `isFrontCamera` value, as shown in the preceding code, and set the toast message to notify the user.

With this, we have successfully built our own version of a face detection application!

HOG descriptors

Histogram of Oriented Gradients (HOG) descriptors are feature descriptors that use the direction of intensity of the gradients and edge directions. For HOG descriptors, we divide the image into small cells, compute a histogram for each cell, and further combine these histograms to compute one single descriptor. They are similar to SIFT descriptors in the sense that both use image gradients and both divide the image into spatial bins and form a histogram, but SIFT descriptors help you to match local regions (using keypoint locations), while HOG descriptors use sliding windows to detect objects. The HOG descriptor works well with geometric and illumination transformations, but does not work well with object orientations (unlike SIFT, which works well with change in orientations).

The HOG descriptor is divided into multiple steps:

*   **Computing gradient**: We first calculate the gradient values for all the pixels in the image using any derivative mask over the image in horizontal and vertical directions (you can choose from either one direction or both directions). Some common derivative masks are the Sobel operator, Prewitt operator, and the likes, but the original algorithm recommends that you use a 1D derivative mask, that is, [-1, 0, +1].

- **Orientation binning**: Create a histogram of the weighted gradients that were computed in the previous step. The gradient values are divided into bin values, ranging from 0 to 180, or 0 to 360 (depending on whether we are using signed or unsigned gradient values).

- **Combining cells to form blocks**: After computing histograms for each cell, we combine these cells into blocks and form a combined histogram of the block using its constituent cell's normalized histograms. The final HOG descriptor is a vector of the normalized histograms.

- **Building the classifier**: In the final step of the algorithm, feed the HOG feature vectors that were computed in the previous step in to your favorite learning algorithm, and build a model that will later be used to detect objects in images:

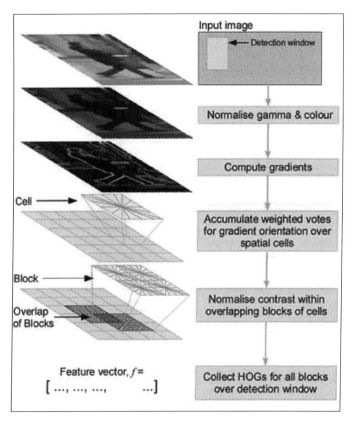

Flowchart of a HOG Descriptor

Let's now take a look at an Android application that detects objects using HOG descriptors.

Since OpenCV provides a pretrained HOG descriptor to detect people in images, we will write an Android application that can detect people in images (we won't have to train our descriptor). Since the calculations involved in computing HOG descriptors are expensive, making a real-time application for a mobile platform with limited computational resources turns out to be a difficult task. So instead, we will build an application that will only detect people in single images.

For this, let's refer to *Chapter 2*, *Detecting Basic Features in Images*, where we built an application that could read images from your phone's gallery and perform any operation based on the user's choice (hopefully, you still have that project saved somewhere in your computer). We won't need the entire application. We will only take the base of that application and make a new function to detect people in any image from the gallery.

If you have the project from *Chapter 2*, *Detecting Basic Features in Images*, saved, make the following changes to it. Add a new menu option *Detect Face* to the application menu (refer to *Chapter 2*, *Detecting Basic Features in Images*), and in the `onSelectedOptionItem()` function, add the following lines:

```
else if (id == R.id.FaceDetect) {
        //Detec Faces
        HOGDescriptor();
    }
```

Make a new function `HOGDescriptor()`, where we'll implement people detection as follows:

```
void HOGDescriptor() {
        Mat grayMat = new Mat();
        Mat people = new Mat();

        //Converting the image to grayscale
        Imgproc.cvtColor(originalMat, grayMat,
          Imgproc.COLOR_BGR2GRAY);

        HOGDescriptor hog = new HOGDescriptor();
        hog.setSVMDetector(HOGDescriptor
          .getDefaultPeopleDetector());

        MatOfRect faces = new MatOfRect();
        MatOfDouble weights = new MatOfDouble();

        hog.detectMultiScale(grayMat, faces, weights);
        originalMat.copyTo(people);
        //Draw faces on the image
        Rect[] facesArray = faces.toArray();
```

```
for (int i = 0; i < facesArray.length; i++)
    Core.rectangle(people, facesArray[i].tl(),
        facesArray[i].br(), new Scalar(100), 3);

//Converting Mat back to Bitmap
Utils.matToBitmap(people, currentBitmap);
loadImageToImageView();
}
```

In the preceding code snippet, we first convert the image to a grayscale image. Then, we initialize `HOGDescriptor` with a pretrained model (using SVM) using the following lines:

```
HOGDescriptor hog = new HOGDescriptor();
hog.setSVMDetector(HOGDescriptor.getDefaultPeopleDetector());
```

The next step is simple; we will call the `detectMultiScale()` function, which will return all the faces in the image. The second parameter in the function stores the regions where people were detected. We will then iterate through all such regions and draw rectangles around them on the image.

Project – Happy Camera

Practice is better than theory. It's time to apply your learning from this chapter and build a cool camera application, which automatically clicks a picture when it detects smiling faces.

The trick is that we will use two different types of cascade classifiers. First, we will use Haar cascades to find faces on the image and store the positions of all the faces. Then we will use the Haar cascades to detect smiles in an image and store them. Now we try to match the face with a smile. For each smile, we find the corresponding face in the image. This is simple: if the smiling region is within any detected face region, we say that it's a match.

After locating all the smiling faces in the image, find the ratio of the smiling faces to all faces to nonsmiling faces, and if that ratio is greater than a certain threshold we say that it's a happy picture and click the image. Though one thing to note here is the ratio that we are using. We can use a different metric to tag an image as a happy image. If we calculate the ratio of smiling faces to total faces, there is a problem that if you have just two people in the image and one of them is not smiling (or has a standard expression), then our application will not click an image. Hence, to avoid such situations, we choose to have a relaxed ratio of smiling faces to nonsmiling faces in order to classify images as happy images.

How do we go about building this application? Most parts of the application have already been discussed in this chapter. The remaining parts of the application are as follows:

1. **Adding a smile detector**: This is very simple. It is exactly the same as what we did to detect faces; instead here, we will use Haar cascades for smiles. You can find a pretrained model at `https://github.com/Itseez/opencv/blob/master/data/haarcascades/haarcascade_smile.xml`.

2. **Correlating faces and smiles**: Once we have faces and smiles, we need to find matching pairs of faces and smiles in the image. Why do we want to correlate them? Why not use the number of smiles directly? Yes, we can do that. It is not necessary to correlate faces and smiles. The only advantage of doing this extra step is to reduce the false positives. If there is no corresponding face for a smile, we can choose to ignore that smile in our calculations.

3. **Tagging happy images**: Once you have the face and smile pairs ready, calculate the ratio (explained earlier) and make a decision on whether you want to save that image or not.

4. **Actually saving the image**: After tagging the image as a happy image, make a function that will actually save the image to your phone.

You just made a cool camera application!

Only after you have tried to build this application yourself, you can take a look at a sample implementation from the code bundle that accompanies this book.

Summary

This chapter was a continuation of the last chapter, where we saw some basic feature detection algorithms. Here we have learnt a few more algorithms that can be used in face, eye, and person detection. Cascade classifiers are a type of supervised learning models, where we first train a classifier with some labelled data, and then use the trained model to detect new unencountered data.

In the coming chapters, we will take a look at topics such as image stitching and how to use machine learning in computer vision algorithms.

5
Tracking Objects in Videos

Object tracking is one of the most important applications of computer vision. It can be used for many applications, some of which are as follows:

- Human–computer interaction: We might want to track the position of a person's finger and use its motion to control the cursor on our machines
- Surveillance: Street cameras can capture pedestrians' motions that can be tracked to detect suspicious activities
- Video stabilization and compression
- Statistics in sports: By tracking a player's movement in a game of football, we can provide statistics such as distance travelled, heat maps, and so on

In this chapter, you will learn the following topics:

- Optical flow
- Image Pyramids
- Global Motion Estimation
- The KLT tracker

Optical flow

Optical flow is an algorithm that detects the pattern of the motion of objects, or edges, between consecutive frames in a video. This motion may be caused by the motion of the object or the motion of the camera. Optical flow is a vector that depicts the motion of a point from the first frame to the second.

The optical flow algorithm works under two basic assumptions:

- The pixel intensities are almost constant between consecutive frames
- The neighboring pixels have the same motion as the anchor pixel

We can represent the intensity of a pixel in any frame by $f(x,y,t)$. Here, the parameter t represents the frame in a video. Let's assume that, in the next dt time, the pixel moves by (dx,dy). Since we have assumed that the intensity doesn't change in consecutive frames, we can say:

$f(x,y,t) = f(x + dx, y + dy, t + dt)$

Now we take the Taylor series expansion of the RHS in the preceding equation:

$$f(x,y,t) = f(x,y,t) + \frac{\partial f}{\partial x} dx + \frac{\partial f}{\partial y} dy + \frac{\partial f}{\partial t} dt$$

Cancelling the common term, we get:

$$f_x\, dx + f_y\, dy + f_t\, dt = 0$$

Where $f_x = \dfrac{\partial f}{\partial x}; f_y = \dfrac{\partial f}{\partial y}$.

Dividing both sides of the equation by dt we get:

$$f_x u + f_y v + f_t = 0$$

This equation is called the optical flow equation. Rearranging the equation we get:

$$v = -\frac{f_x}{f_y} u - \frac{f_t}{f_y}$$

We can see that this represents the equation of a line in the (u,v) plane. However, with only one equation available and two unknowns, this problem is under constraint at the moment. Two of the most widely used methods to calculate the optical flow are explained in the upcoming section.

The Horn and Schunck method

By taking into account our assumptions, we get:

$$\iint \left\{ \left(f_x u + f_y v + f_t \right)^2 + \lambda \left(u_x^2 + u_y^2 + v_x^2 + v_y^2 \right) \right\} dx\ dy$$

We can say that the first term will be small due to our assumption that the brightness is constant between consecutive frames. So, the square of this term will be even smaller. The second term corresponds to the assumption that the neighboring pixels have similar motion to the anchor pixel. We need to minimize the preceding equation. For this, we differentiate the preceding equation with respect to u and v. We get the following equations:

$$\left(f_x u + f_y v + f_t \right) f_x + \lambda \left(\Delta^2 u \right) = 0$$

$$\left(f_x u + f_y v + f_t \right) f_y + \lambda \left(\Delta^2 v \right) = 0$$

Here, $\Delta^2 u$ and $\Delta^2 v$ are the Laplacians of u and v respectively.

The Lucas and Kanade method

We start off with the optical flow equation that we derived earlier and noticed that it is under constrained as it has one equation and two variables:

$$f_x u + f_y v + f_t = 0$$

To overcome this problem, we make use of the assumption that pixels in a 3x3 neighborhood have the same optical flow:

$$f_{x1} u + f_{y1} v + f_{t1} = 0$$
$$f_{x2} u + f_{y2} v + f_{t2} = 0$$
$$\vdots$$
$$f_{x9} u + f_{y9} v + f_{t9} = 0$$

We can rewrite these equations in the form of matrices, as shown here:

$$\begin{bmatrix} f_{x1} & f_{y1} \\ \vdots & \vdots \\ f_{x9} & f_{y9} \end{bmatrix} \begin{bmatrix} u \\ v \end{bmatrix} = \begin{bmatrix} -f_{t1} \\ \vdots \\ -f_{t9} \end{bmatrix}$$

This can be rewritten in the form:

$$AU = b$$

Where:

$$A = \begin{bmatrix} f_{x1} & f_{y1} \\ \vdots & \vdots \\ f_{x9} & f_{y9} \end{bmatrix}; \quad U = \begin{bmatrix} u \\ v \end{bmatrix}; \quad b = \begin{bmatrix} -f_{t1} \\ \vdots \\ -f_{t9} \end{bmatrix}$$

As we can see, A is a 9x2 matrix, U is a 2x1 matrix, and b is a 9x1 matrix. Ideally, to solve for U, we just need to multiply by A^{-1} on both sides of the equation. However, this is not possible, as we can only take the inverse of square matrices. Thus, we try to transform A into a square matrix by first multiplying the equation by A^T on both sides of the equation:

$$\left(A^T A\right)U = A^T b$$

Now $A^T A$ is a square matrix of dimension 2x2. Hence, we can take its inverse:

$$u = \left(A^T A\right)^{-1} A^T b$$

On solving this equation, we get:

$$\begin{bmatrix} u \\ v \end{bmatrix} = \begin{bmatrix} \sum_i f_{xi}^2 & \sum_i f_{xi} f_{yi} \\ \sum_i f_{xi} f_{yi} & \sum_i f_{yi}^2 \end{bmatrix}^{-1} \begin{bmatrix} -\sum_i f_{xi} f_{ti} \\ -\sum_i f_{yi} f_{ti} \end{bmatrix}$$

This method of multiplying the transpose and then taking an inverse is called **pseudo-inverse**.

This equation can also be obtained by finding the minimum of the following equation:

$$\sum_i \left(f_{xi}u + f_{yi}v + f_{ti} \right)^2$$

According to the optical flow equation and our assumptions, this value should be equal to zero. Since the neighborhood pixels do not have exactly the same values as the anchor pixel, this value is very small. This method is called **Least Square Error**. To solve for the minimum, we differentiate this equation with respect to u and v, and equate it to zero. We get the following equations:

$$\sum_i \left(f_{xi}u + f_{yi}v + f_{ti} \right) f_{xi} = 0$$

$$\sum_i \left(f_{xi}u + f_{yi}v + f_{ti} \right) f_{yi} = 0$$

Now we have two equations and two variables, so this system of equations can be solved. We rewrite the preceding equations as follows:

$$\sum_i f_{xi}^2 u + \sum_i f_{xi} f_{yi} v = -\sum_i f_{xi} f_{ti}$$

$$\sum_i f_{xi} f_{yi} u + \sum_i f_{yi}^2 v = -\sum_i f_{yi} f_{ti}$$

So, by arranging these equations in the form of a matrix, we get the same equation as obtained earlier:

$$\begin{bmatrix} \sum_i f_{xi}^2 & \sum_i f_{xi} f_{yi} \\ \sum_i f_{xi} f_{yi} & \sum_i f_{yi}^2 \end{bmatrix} \begin{bmatrix} u \\ v \end{bmatrix} = \begin{bmatrix} -\sum_i f_{xi} f_{ti} \\ -\sum_i f_{yi} f_{ti} \end{bmatrix}$$

Since, the matrix A is now a 2x2 matrix, it is possible to take an inverse. On taking the inverse, the equation obtained is as follows:

$$\begin{bmatrix} u \\ v \end{bmatrix} = \begin{bmatrix} \sum_i f_{xi}^{2} & \sum_i f_{xi} f_{yi} \\ \sum_i f_{xi} f_{yi} & \sum_i f_{yi}^{2} \end{bmatrix}^{-1} \begin{bmatrix} -\sum_i f_{xi} f_{ti} \\ -\sum_i f_{yi} f_{ti} \end{bmatrix}$$

This can be simplified as:

$$\begin{bmatrix} u \\ v \end{bmatrix} = \frac{1}{\sum_i f_{xi}^{2} \sum_i f_{yi}^{2} - \left(\sum_i f_{xi} f_{yi}\right)^2} \begin{bmatrix} \sum_i f_{yi}^{2} & -\sum_i f_{xi} f_{yi} \\ \sum_i f_{xi} f_{yi} & \sum_i f_{xi}^{2} \end{bmatrix}^{-1} \begin{bmatrix} -\sum_i f_{xi} f_{ti} \\ -\sum_i f_{yi} f_{ti} \end{bmatrix}$$

Solving for u and v, we get:

$$u = \frac{\sum_i f_{xi} f_{yi} \sum_i f_{yi} f_{ti} - \sum_i f_{yi}^{2} \sum_i f_{xi} f_{ti}}{\sum_i f_{xi}^{2} \sum_i f_{yi}^{2} - \left(\sum_i f_{xi} f_{yi}\right)^2}$$

$$v = \frac{\sum_i f_{xi} f_{yi} \sum_i f_{xi} f_{ti} - \sum_i f_{xi}^{2} \sum_i f_{yi} f_{ti}}{\sum_i f_{xi}^{2} \sum_i f_{yi}^{2} - \left(\sum_i f_{xi} f_{yi}\right)^2}$$

Now we have the values for all the f_{xi}'s, f_{yi}'s, and f_{ti}'s. Thus, we can find the values of u and v for each pixel.

When we implement this algorithm, it is observed that the optical flow is not very smooth near the edges of the objects. This is due to the brightness constraint not being satisfied. To overcome this situation, we use **image pyramids** (explained in detail in the following sections).

Checking out the optical flow on Android

To see the optical flow in action on Android, we will create a grid of points over a video feed from the camera, and then the lines will be drawn for each point that will depict the motion of the point on the video, which is superimposed by the point on the grid.

Before we begin, we will set up our project to use OpenCV and obtain the feed from the camera. We will process the frames to calculate the optical flow.

First, create a new project in Android Studio, in the same way as we did in the previous chapters. We will set the activity name to `MainActivity.java` and the XML resource file as `activity_main.xml`. Second, we will give the app the permissions to access the camera. In the `AndroidManifest.xml` file, add the following lines to the manifest tag:

```
<uses-permission android:name="android.permission.CAMERA" />
```

Make sure that your activity tag for `MainActivity` contains the following line as an attribute:

```
android:screenOrientation="landscape"
```

Our `activity_main.xml` file will contain a simple `JavaCameraView`. This is a custom OpenCV defined layout that enables us to access the camera frames and processes them as normal `Mat` objects. The XML code has been shown here:

```
<LinearLayout xmlns:android="http://schemas.android.com/apk/res/
android"
    xmlns:tools="http://schemas.android.com/tools"
    android:layout_width="match_parent"
    android:layout_height="match_parent"
    android:orientation="horizontal">

    <org.opencv.android.JavaCameraView
        android:layout_width="fill_parent"
        android:layout_height="fill_parent"
        android:id="@+id/main_activity_surface_view" />

</LinearLayout>
```

Now, let's work on some Java code. First, we'll define some global variables that we will use later in the code or for other sections in this chapter:

```java
private static final String    TAG = "com.packtpub.
masteringopencvandroid.chapter5.MainActivity";

    private static final int        VIEW_MODE_KLT_TRACKER = 0;
    private static final int        VIEW_MODE_OPTICAL_FLOW = 1;

    private int                     mViewMode;
    private Mat                     mRgba;
    private Mat                     mIntermediateMat;
    private Mat                     mGray;
    private Mat                     mPrevGray;

    MatOfPoint2f prevFeatures, nextFeatures;
    MatOfPoint features;

    MatOfByte status;
    MatOfFloat err;

    private MenuItem                mItemPreviewOpticalFlow,
mItemPreviewKLT;

    private CameraBridgeViewBase    mOpenCvCameraView;
```

We will need to create a callback function for OpenCV, like we did earlier. In addition to the code we used earlier, we will also enable `CameraView` to capture frames for processing:

```java
private BaseLoaderCallback  mLoaderCallback = new
BaseLoaderCallback(this) {
        @Override
        public void onManagerConnected(int status) {
            switch (status) {
                case LoaderCallbackInterface.SUCCESS:
                {
                    Log.i(TAG, "OpenCV loaded successfully");

                    mOpenCvCameraView.enableView();
                } break;
                default:
                {
```

```
                    super.onManagerConnected(status);
                } break;
            }
        }
    };
```

We will now check whether the OpenCV manager is installed on the phone, which contains the required libraries. In the onResume function, add the following line of code:

```
OpenCVLoader.initAsync(OpenCVLoader.OPENCV_VERSION_2_4_10,
    this, mLoaderCallback);
```

In the onCreate() function, add the following line before calling setContentView to prevent the screen from turning off, while using the app:

```
getWindow().addFlags(WindowManager.LayoutParams.
    FLAG_KEEP_SCREEN_ON);
```

We will now initialize our JavaCameraView object. Add the following lines after setContentView has been called:

```
mOpenCvCameraView = (CameraBridgeViewBase)
    findViewById(R.id.main_activity_surface_view);
mOpenCvCameraView.setCvCameraViewListener(this);
```

Notice that we called setCvCameraViewListener with the this parameter. For this, we need to make our activity implement the CvCameraViewListener2 interface. So, your class definition for the MainActivity class should look like the following code:

```
public class MainActivity extends Activity
    implements CvCameraViewListener2
```

We will add a menu to this activity to toggle between different examples in this chapter. Add the following lines to the onCreateOptionsMenu function:

```
mItemPreviewKLT = menu.add("KLT Tracker");
mItemPreviewOpticalFlow = menu.add("Optical Flow");
```

We will now add some actions to the menu items. In the onOptionsItemSelected function, add the following lines:

```
if (item == mItemPreviewOpticalFlow) {
        mViewMode = VIEW_MODE_OPTICAL_FLOW;
        resetVars();
```

```
    } else if (item == mItemPreviewKLT) {
        mViewMode = VIEW_MODE_KLT_TRACKER;
        resetVars();
    }

    return true;
```

We used a `resetVars` function to reset all the `Mat` objects. It has been defined as follows:

```
private void resetVars() {
    mPrevGray = new Mat(mGray.rows(), mGray.cols(), CvType.
CV_8UC1);
    features = new MatOfPoint();
    prevFeatures = new MatOfPoint2f();
    nextFeatures = new MatOfPoint2f();
    status = new MatOfByte();
    err = new MatOfFloat();
}
```

We will also add the code to make sure that the camera is released for use by other applications, whenever our application is suspended or killed. So, add the following snippet of code to the `onPause` and `onDestroy` functions:

```
if (mOpenCvCameraView != null)
        mOpenCvCameraView.disableView();
```

After the OpenCV camera has been started, the `onCameraViewStarted` function is called, which is where we will add all our object initializations:

```
public void onCameraViewStarted(int width, int height) {
    mRgba = new Mat(height, width, CvType.CV_8UC4);
    mIntermediateMat = new Mat(height, width, CvType.CV_8UC4);
    mGray = new Mat(height, width, CvType.CV_8UC1);
    resetVars();
}
```

Similarly, the `onCameraViewStopped` function is called when we stop capturing frames. Here we will release all the objects we created when the view was started:

```
public void onCameraViewStopped() {
    mRgba.release();
    mGray.release();
    mIntermediateMat.release();
}
```

Now we will add the implementation to process each frame of the feed that we captured from the camera. OpenCV calls the onCameraFrame method for each frame, with the frame as a parameter. We will use this to process each frame. We will use the viewMode variable to distinguish between the optical flow and the KLT tracker, and have different case constructs for the two:

```
public Mat onCameraFrame(CvCameraViewFrame inputFrame) {
        final int viewMode = mViewMode;
        switch (viewMode) {
            case VIEW_MODE_OPTICAL_FLOW:
```

We will use the gray() function to obtain the Mat object that contains the captured frame in a grayscale format. OpenCV also provides a similar function called rgba() to obtain a colored frame. Then we will check whether this is the first run. If this is the first run, we will create and fill up a features array that stores the position of all the points in a grid, where we will compute the optical flow:

```
                mGray = inputFrame.gray();
                if(features.toArray().length==0){
                    int rowStep = 50, colStep = 100;
                    int nRows = mGray.rows()/rowStep, nCols = mGray.cols()/colStep;

                    Point points[] = new Point[nRows*nCols];
                    for(int i=0; i<nRows; i++){
                        for(int j=0; j<nCols; j++){
                            points[i*nCols+j]=new Point(j*colStep, i*rowStep);
                        }
                    }

                    features.fromArray(points);

                    prevFeatures.fromList(features.toList());
                    mPrevGray = mGray.clone();
                    break;
                }
```

The `mPrevGray` object refers to the previous frame in a grayscale format. We copied the points to a `prevFeatures` object that we will use to calculate the optical flow and store the corresponding points in the next frame in `nextFeatures`. All of the computation is carried out in the `calcOpticalFlowPyrLK` OpenCV defined function. This function takes in the grayscale version of the previous frame, the current grayscale frame, an object that contains the feature points whose optical flow needs to be calculated, and an object that will store the position of the corresponding points in the current frame:

```
nextFeatures.fromArray(prevFeatures.toArray());
Video.calcOpticalFlowPyrLK(mPrevGray, mGray,
    prevFeatures, nextFeatures, status, err);
```

Now, we have the position of the grid of points and their position in the next frame as well. So, we will now draw a line that depicts the motion of each point on the grid:

```
List<Point> prevList=features.toList(),
nextList=nextFeatures.toList();
Scalar color = new Scalar(255);

for(int i = 0; i<prevList.size(); i++){
    Core.line(mGray, prevList.get(i), nextList.get(i),
color);
    }
```

Before the loop ends, we have to copy the current frame to `mPrevGray` so that we can calculate the optical flow in the subsequent frames:

```
mPrevGray = mGray.clone();
break;
default: mViewMode = VIEW_MODE_OPTICAL_FLOW;
```

After we end the switch case construct, we will return a Mat object. This is the image that will be displayed as an output to the user of the application. Here, since all our operations and processing were performed on the grayscale image, we will return this image:

```
return mGray;
```

So, this is all about optical flow. The result can be seen in the following image:

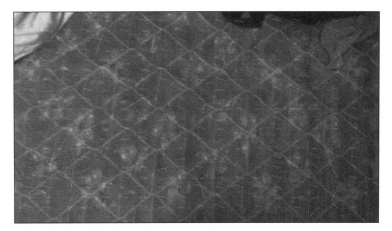

Optical flow at various points in the camera feed

Image pyramids

Pyramids are multiple copies of the same images that differ in their sizes. They are represented as layers, as shown in the following figure. Each level in the pyramid is obtained by reducing the rows and columns by half. Thus, effectively, we make the image's size one quarter of its original size:

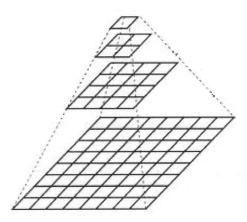

Relative sizes of pyramids

Pyramids intrinsically define **reduce** and **expand** as their two operations. Reduce refers to a reduction in the image's size, whereas expand refers to an increase in its size.

 We will use a convention that lower levels in a pyramid mean downsized images and higher levels mean upsized images.

Gaussian pyramids

In the reduce operation, the equation that we use to successively find levels in pyramids, while using a 5x5 sliding window, has been written as follows. Notice that the size of the image reduces to a quarter of its original size:

$$g_l(i,j) = \sum_{m=-2}^{2} \sum_{n=-2}^{2} w(m,n) g_{l-1}(2i+m, 2j+n)$$

The elements of the weight kernel, w, should add up to 1. We use a 5x5 Gaussian kernel for this task. This operation is similar to convolution with the exception that the resulting image doesn't have the same size as the original image. The following image shows you the reduce operation:

The reduce operation

The expand operation is the reverse process of reduce. We try to generate images of a higher size from images that belong to lower layers. Thus, the resulting image is blurred and is of a lower resolution. The equation we use to perform expansion is as follows:

$$g_{l,n}(i,j) = \sum_{m=-2}^{2} \sum_{n=-2}^{2} w(m,n) g_{l,n-1}\left(\frac{i-m}{2}, \frac{j-n}{2}\right)$$

The weight kernel in this case, w, is the same as the one used to perform the reduce operation. The following image shows you the expand operation:

The expand operation

The weights are calculated using the Gaussian function that we used in *Chapter 1, Applying Effects to Images*, to perform Gaussian blur.

Laplacian pyramids

Laplacian pyramids are images that generally represent the edges. They are obtained from Gaussian pyramids. They are calculated using the following formula:

$$L_i = g_i - Expand\left(g_{i+1}\right)$$

g_i and $Expand\left(g_{i+1}\right)$ are not the same once we downsize an image; we lose information, which cannot be recovered.

Gaussian and Laplacian pyramids in OpenCV

To see how pyramids are created in OpenCV, we will create two new activities called `PyramidActivity` and `HomeActivity`. The `PyramidActivity` class will load an image from the gallery, and then, based on the user's options, perform the required actions. `HomeActivity` is used to call either `PyramidActivity` or `MainActivity` based on options provided by the user. So first, we make the resource for the `HomeActivity` class and call it `activity_home.xml`:

```xml
<?xml version="1.0" encoding="utf-8"?>

<ScrollView
    xmlns:android="http://schemas.android.com/apk/res/android"
    android:layout_width="match_parent"
```

```
        android:layout_height="match_parent" >
    <LinearLayout
        android:layout_height="match_parent"
        android:layout_width="match_parent"
        android:orientation="vertical" >

        <Button
            android:id="@+id/bPyramids"
            android:layout_height="wrap_content"
            android:layout_width="wrap_content"
            android:text="Image Pyramids" />

        <Button
            android:id="@+id/bOptFlowKLT"
            android:layout_height="wrap_content"
            android:layout_width="wrap_content"
            android:text="Optical Flow and KLT Tracker" />

    </LinearLayout>
</ScrollView>
```

In our Java code, we will add listeners to these buttons to call the respective activities, as follows:

```
Button bPyramids, bOptFlowKLT;
        bPyramids = (Button) findViewById(R.id.bPyramids);
        bOptFlowKLT = (Button) findViewById(R.id.bOptFlowKLT);
        bOptFlowKLT.setOnClickListener(new View.OnClickListener() {
            @Override
            public void onClick(View v) {
                Intent i = new Intent(getApplicationContext(),
MainActivity.class);
                startActivity(i);
            }
        });
        bPyramids.setOnClickListener(new View.OnClickListener() {
            @Override
            public void onClick(View v) {
                Intent i = new Intent(getApplicationContext(),
PyramidActivity.class);
                startActivity(i);
            }
        });
```

Now we move on to the implementation of `PyramidActivity`. First, we will take a look at `activity_pyramid.xml`. We will add buttons to perform various actions as per the user's options. The possible options are Gaussian pyramid up, Gaussian pyramid down, and Laplacian pyramid calculation. The following code is inserted into `LinearLayout` inside `ScrollView`:

```
<ImageView
        android:layout_width="match_parent"
        android:layout_height="0dp"
        android:layout_weight="0.5"
        android:id="@+id/ivImage" />
    <LinearLayout
        android:layout_width="match_parent"
        android:layout_height="wrap_content"
        android:orientation="horizontal">
        <Button
            android:layout_width="match_parent"
            android:layout_height="wrap_content"
            android:layout_weight="0.5"
            android:id="@+id/bGaussianPyrUp"
            android:text="Gaussian Pyramid Up"/>
        <Button
            android:layout_width="match_parent"
            android:layout_height="wrap_content"
            android:layout_weight="0.5"
            android:id="@+id/bGaussianPyrDown"
            android:text="Gaussian Pyramid Down"/>
    </LinearLayout>

    <LinearLayout
        android:layout_width="match_parent"
        android:layout_height="wrap_content"
        android:orientation="horizontal">
        <Button
            android:layout_width="match_parent"
            android:layout_height="wrap_content"
            android:id="@+id/bLaplacianPyr"
            android:text="Laplacian Pyramid"/>
    </LinearLayout>
```

We will also have a menu file for this activity that will be used to load images from the gallery. We will have a similar method to load images from the gallery that we did in the earlier chapters. We will have the following lines in `PyramidActivity.java`:

```
@Override
    public boolean onCreateOptionsMenu(Menu menu) {
        getMenuInflater().inflate(R.menu.menu_pyramid, menu);
        return true;
    }

    @Override
    public boolean onOptionsItemSelected(MenuItem item) {
        int id = item.getItemId();

        if (id == R.id.action_load_first_image) {
            Intent photoPickerIntent = new Intent(Intent.ACTION_PICK);
            photoPickerIntent.setType("image/*");
            startActivityForResult(photoPickerIntent, SELECT_PHOTO);
            return true;
        }

        return super.onOptionsItemSelected(item);
    }
```

Now we will define some global variables that we will need:

```
private final int SELECT_PHOTO = 1;
private ImageView ivImage;
Mat src;
static int ACTION_MODE = 0;
static final int MODE_NONE = 0, MODE_GAUSSIAN_PYR_UP = 1,
  MODE_GAUSSIAN_PYR_DOWN = 2, MODE_LAPLACIAN_PYR = 3;
private boolean srcSelected = false;
Button bGaussianPyrUp, bGaussianPyrDown, bLaplacianPyr;
```

We also need to specify the OpenCV callback function and initialize it in `onResume`, as we did earlier.

In our `onCreate` function, after we initialize all our buttons, we will first disable them until an image has been loaded from the gallery. So, add the following lines after initializing all the buttons in this activity:

```
bGaussianPyrDown.setEnabled(false);
bGaussianPyrUp.setEnabled(false);
bLaplacianPyr.setEnabled(false);
```

In our `onActivityResult`, we will check whether the image has been loaded successfully, and if it has been we activate the buttons. We also load the image to a Mat and store it for later use:

```
switch(requestCode) {
            case SELECT_PHOTO:
                if(resultCode == RESULT_OK){
                    try {
                        final Uri imageUri =
                            imageReturnedIntent.getData();
                        final InputStream imageStream =
                            getContentResolver().
                            openInputStream(imageUri);
                        final Bitmap selectedImage =
                            BitmapFactory.decodeStream(imageStream);
                        src = new Mat(selectedImage.getHeight(),
                            selectedImage.getWidth(),
                            CvType.CV_8UC4);
                        Utils.bitmapToMat(selectedImage, src);
                        srcSelected = true;
                        bGaussianPyrUp.setEnabled(true);
                        bGaussianPyrDown.setEnabled(true);
                        bLaplacianPyr.setEnabled(true);
                    } catch (FileNotFoundException e) {
                        e.printStackTrace();
                    }
                }
                break;
        }
```

Now we will add the listeners for each of the buttons. In your `onCreate`, add the following lines:

```
bGaussianPyrUp.setOnClickListener(new View.OnClickListener() {
        @Override
        public void onClick(View v) {
            ACTION_MODE = MODE_GAUSSIAN_PYR_UP;
            executeTask();
        }
    });

bGaussianPyrDown.setOnClickListener(new View.OnClickListener() {
        @Override
        public void onClick(View v) {
```

```
            ACTION_MODE = MODE_GAUSSIAN_PYR_DOWN;
            executeTask();
        }
    });

bLaplacianPyr.setOnClickListener(new View.OnClickListener() {
        @Override
        public void onClick(View v) {
            ACTION_MODE = MODE_LAPLACIAN_PYR;
            executeTask();
        }
    });
```

Now we will implement the `executeTask` function that will perform the required computations in `AsyncTask`, and after they are completed, they will be loaded into `ImageView` that we have in our layout:

```
private void executeTask(){
        if(srcSelected){

            new AsyncTask<Void, Void, Bitmap>() {
                @Override
                protected void onPreExecute() {
                    super.onPreExecute();
                }

                @Override
                protected Bitmap doInBackground(Void... params) {
                    Mat srcRes = new Mat();
                    switch (ACTION_MODE){
                        case MODE_GAUSSIAN_PYR_UP:
                            Imgproc.pyrUp(src, srcRes);
                            break;
                        case MODE_GAUSSIAN_PYR_DOWN:
                            Imgproc.pyrDown(src, srcRes);
                            break;
                        case MODE_LAPLACIAN_PYR:
                            Imgproc.pyrDown(src, srcRes);
                            Imgproc.pyrUp(srcRes, srcRes);
                            Core.absdiff(src, srcRes, srcRes);
                            break;
                    }
```

```
            if(ACTION_MODE != 0) {
                Bitmap image =
                    Bitmap.createBitmap(srcRes.cols(),
                    srcRes.rows(), Bitmap.Config.ARGB_8888);

                Utils.matToBitmap(srcRes, image);
                return image;
            }
            return null;
        }

        @Override
        protected void onPostExecute(Bitmap bitmap) {
            super.onPostExecute(bitmap);
            if(bitmap!=null) {
                ivImage.setImageBitmap(bitmap);
            }
        }
    }.execute();
    }
}
```

Here, we have called `pyrUp` and `pyrDown` with just two arguments; however, you can specify a custom size for the results by calling the function as `Imgproc.pyrUp(srcMat, dstMat, resultSize)`.

OpenCV doesn't provide a separate function to calculate the Laplacian pyramid, but we can use the Gaussian pyramids to generate our Laplacian pyramids.

Basic 2D transformations

An object in 3D space can cast a projection in 2D space that is different from the original projection. Such transformations are called 2D transformations. They are shown in the following image. We will use some of these transformations to explain concepts discussed later in the chapter and also in other chapters:

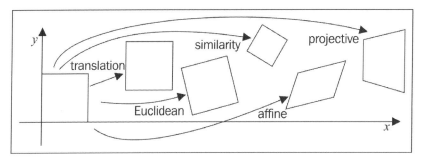

We write these transformations in the mathematical form, along with their matrix representations, as shown here:

- **Translation**: The mathematical representation of a translation transformation is given by:

$$x_{new} = x + x_1$$
$$y_{new} = y + y_1$$

$$T = \begin{bmatrix} 1 & 0 & x_1 \\ 0 & 1 & y_1 \end{bmatrix} \begin{bmatrix} x \\ y \\ 1 \end{bmatrix}$$

- **Affine**: The mathematical representation of an affine transformation is given by:

$$x_{new} = a_1 x + a_2 y + x_1$$
$$y_{new} = b_1 x + b_2 y + y_1$$

$$T = \begin{bmatrix} a_1 & a_2 & x_1 \\ b_1 & b_2 & y_1 \end{bmatrix} \begin{bmatrix} x \\ y \\ 1 \end{bmatrix}$$

- **Rigid**: The mathematical representation of a rigid transformation is given by:

$$x_{new} = \cos\theta x - \sin\theta y + x_1$$
$$y_{new} = \sin\theta x + \cos\theta y + y_1$$

$$T = \begin{bmatrix} \cos\theta & -\sin\theta & x_1 \\ \sin\theta & \cos\theta & y_1 \end{bmatrix} \begin{bmatrix} x \\ y \\ 1 \end{bmatrix}$$

- **Projective**: The mathematical representation of a projective transformation is given by:

$$x_{new} = \frac{a_1 x + a_2 y + x_1}{c_1 x + c_2 y + 1}$$

$$y_{new} = \frac{b_1 x + b_2 y + x_1}{c_1 x + c_2 y + 1}$$

Global motion estimation

Global motion estimation, as the name suggests, is the detection of motion using all pixels in a frame in its calculation. Some of the applications of global motion estimation include:

- Video stabilization
- Video encoding/decoding
- Object segmentation

This method was proposed by Bergen et.al. (1992). In this method, when the distance between the camera and the background scenes is large, we can approximate the motion of objects as affine transformations. The equations we saw earlier were as follows:

$$x_{new} = a_1 x + a_2 y + x_1$$

$$y_{new} = b_1 x + b_2 y + x_1$$

We can rewrite these equations in the matrix form as follows:

$$\begin{bmatrix} x_{new} \\ y_{new} \end{bmatrix} = \begin{bmatrix} x & y & 1 & 0 & 0 & 0 \\ 0 & 0 & 0 & x & y & 1 \end{bmatrix} \begin{bmatrix} a_1 \\ a_2 \\ x_1 \\ b_1 \\ b_2 \\ y_1 \end{bmatrix}$$

This can be written as $U(x) = X(x)a$.

According to the optical flow equation:

$$f_x u + f_y v + f_t = 0$$

We try to estimate the motion in the image such that all the pixels satisfy it. Thus, we sum up the optical flow equation for all the pixels and try to generate an estimate:

$$E[U] = \sum_X \left(f_t + F^T U \right)^2$$

$$where, \qquad F = \begin{bmatrix} f_x \\ f_y \end{bmatrix}$$

$f_t + F^T U$ should ideally be zero but practically, it is a small value. Thus, the squared error will be small. Hence, we need to minimize it for the best results:

$$E[a] = \sum_X \left(f_t + F^T X a \right)^2$$

$$E[\partial a] = \sum_X \left(f_t + F^T X \partial a \right)^2$$

This equation can be minimized with respect to ∂a to the following linear equation:

$$\left[\sum_X X^T F F^T X \right] \partial a = -\sum_X X^T F f_t$$

This linear equation can be written as:

$$Aa = B$$

This algorithm is now divided into four subparts: pyramid construction, motion estimation, image warping, and coarse-to-fine refinement.

For the pyramid construction, we first take a Gaussian pyramid of the images at time *t* and *t-1*, and compute the global flows iteratively, starting from the smallest layers going toward the bigger layers.

Then, for each layer, to find the motion estimation, we use the linear equation derived earlier to compute A and B for the frames at time *t* and *t-1*, and use this information to compute an estimate for a $\left(\left[a_1 \; a_2 \; x_1 \; b_1 \; b_2 \; y_1\right]^T\right)$. We then warp the image at time *t-1* to an image, which tries to generate the object motion from the original image. This new image is compared to the image captured at time *t*. We then iteratively warp the image frame obtained at *t-1* to compute the value of ∂a. With this value of ∂a, we generate another warped image, which is then compared to the image at time *t*. We use this value of ∂a to update the value of *a*. This process is performed multiple times until we have a good enough estimate of the motion of the image.

Image warping is the process of performing any transformation on an image to produce another image. For this method, we perform affine transformations because of our earlier assumptions:

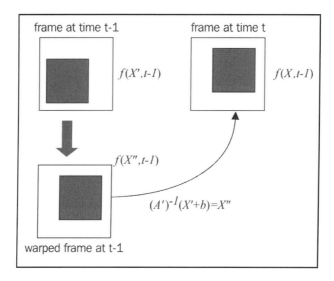

For the final step, coarse-to-fine refinement, we make use of image pyramids to extend our model to include dense images (for example, representing a depth map).

The Kanade-Lucas-Tomasi tracker

Having seen local and global motion estimation, we will now take a look at object tracking. Tracking objects is one of the most important applications of computer vision. The **Kanade-Lucas-Tomasi (KLT)** tracker implements an optical flow to track objects in videos. The steps to implement the algorithm are explained as follows:

1. Detect Harris corners in the first frame of the video.

2. For each detected Harris corner, compute the motion between consecutive frames using the optical flow (translator) and local affine transformation (affine).

3. Now link these motion vectors from frame-to-frame to track the corners.

4. Generate new Harris corners after a specific number of frames (say, 10 to 20) to compensate for new points entering the scene or to discard the ones going out of the scene.

5. Track the new and old Harris points.

Checking out the KLT tracker on OpenCV

As we have seen earlier, the KLT tracker is one of the best algorithms available to track objects in videos. For this example, we will take a feed from the camera, detect some good trackable features, and update these to the new locations, as obtained by the `calcOpticalFlowPyrLK` function. We will just add a new case construct to the code that we wrote for the optical flow:

```
case VIEW_MODE_KLT_TRACKER:
            mGray = inputFrame.gray();

            if(features.toArray().length==0){
                Imgproc.goodFeaturesToTrack(mGray, features,
                    10, 0.01, 10);
                prevFeatures.fromList(features.toList());
                mPrevGray = mGray.clone();
                break;
            }
```

The `goodFeaturesToTrack` function uses the Shi-Tomasi method to calculate good trackable features in an image. This could be replaced by any reliable feature calculation technique. It takes the frame in a grayscale format as the input and returns the list of features. It also takes the parameter of the maximum number of features, to track, the quality of features, and the minimum distance between features respectively. For the purpose of this sample, we will only calculate features in the first frame and track these features in the subsequent frames.

Now we will obtain the optical flow for the feature points obtained previously. Note that `nextFeatures` contains the locations of the corresponding points in the previous frame in `prevFeatures`. We will mark the location of the feature points with circles. Note that we are drawing the circles at the new locations of the features:

```
Video.calcOpticalFlowPyrLK(mPrevGray, mGray,
    prevFeatures, nextFeatures, status, err);
List<Point> drawFeature = nextFeatures.toList();
for(int i = 0; i<drawFeature.size(); i++){
    Point p = drawFeature.get(i);
    Core.circle(mGray, p, 5, new Scalar(255));
}
```

Now we need to set the current frame as the previous frame, and the current feature point locations as the locations of the features in the previous frame so as to enable tracking:

```
mPrevGray = mGray.clone();
prevFeatures.fromList(nextFeatures.toList());
break;
```

The results of Shi-Tomasi tracker and the KLT tracker can be seen in the following image:

The white circles in the following image represent the features that we are tracking:

As it is visible, a small number of points are not tracked properly. For example, consider the feature point at the *L* key. As you can see, in one frame, it is at the *L* key, while in the other frame, it shifts to the key with the semicolon. If you consider the feature points at the *Y* and *J* keys, they remain in their positions. This is because at the keys *Y* and *J*, there are well-defined corners; hence, the feature points are better there.

Summary

In this chapter, we have seen how to detect a local and global motion in a video, and how we can track objects. We have also learned about Gaussian and Laplacian pyramids, and how they can be used to improve the performance of some computer vision tasks.

In the next chapter, we will learn how to align multiple images and how to stitch them together to form a panoramic image.

6
Working with Image Alignment and Stitching

One limitation of cameras is the limited field of view, often shortened to FOV. Field-of-view is the parameter that defines how much information can be captured in one frame obtained by the camera. So, to capture an image that requires a larger field-of-view, we use image stitching. Image stitching is a method of joining multiple images to form a bigger image that represents the information that is consistent with the original images.

In this chapter, we will take a look at the following topics:

- Image stitching
- Image alignment
- Video stabilization
- Stereo vision

Image stitching

There has been a lot of work in image stitching over the years, but we will take a look at the algorithm OpenCV implements internally. Most of it was proposed by Michael Brown and David Lowe. Image stitching is done in the following steps:

1. Find suitable features and match them reliably across the set of images to obtain the relative positioning.

2. Develop the geometry to choose reliable features that are invariant to rotation, scale, and illumination.

3. Match images using the RANSAC algorithm and a probabilistic model for verification.

4. Align the matched images.

5. Render the results to obtain a panoramic image. We use automatic straightening, gain compensation, and multi-band blending to achieve a seamlessly stitched panoramic image, as shown here:

Feature detection and matching

First, we find and match SIFT features between all the images. By doing this, we get the scale and orientation associated with each feature point. With these details, we can form a similarity invariant matrix, where we can make appropriate measurements for calculations. We accumulate local gradients in the orientation histograms to obtain such a frame. By implementing such an algorithm, edges can shift slightly without modifying the descriptor values, thereby providing small levels of affine and shift invariances. The algorithm also proposes to achieve the illumination invariance using gradients to eliminate bias and normalizes the descriptor vector to eliminate the gain.

The algorithm also makes the assumption that a camera only rotates about its optical center. Due to this assumption, we can define rotations along the three primary axes, x, y, and z, as θ_1, θ_2, and θ_3, respectively. We define a vector θ, as $\theta_1, \theta_2, \theta_3$. We also use the focal length, f as a parameter. Thus, we get the pairwise homographies as $\tilde{u}_i = H_{ij}\tilde{u}_j$.

$$H_{ij} = K_i R_i R_j^T K_j^{-1}$$

Here, $\tilde{u}_i$ and $\tilde{u}_j$ are the homographic image positions. u_i is the image position in a 2-dimensional space:

$$\tilde{u}_i = s_j \left[u_i \ 1 \right]$$

The values of K_i and R_i are defined as follows:

$$K_i = \begin{bmatrix} f_i & 0 & 0 \\ 0 & f_i & 0 \\ 0 & 0 & 1 \end{bmatrix}$$

$$R_i = e^{[\theta_i]_X}, \left[\theta_i \right]_X = \begin{bmatrix} 0 & -\theta_{i3} & \theta_{i2} \\ \theta_{i3} & 0 & -\theta_{i1} \\ -\theta_{i2} & \theta_{i1} & 0 \end{bmatrix}$$

As you can see, this representation of R is consistent with the exponential form of depicting rotations. We have included provisions to allow small changes in positions. Hence, we have the following result:

$$\tilde{u}_i = A_{ij} \tilde{u}_j$$

$$A_{ij} = \begin{bmatrix} a_{11} & a_{12} & a_{13} \\ a_{21} & a_{22} & a_{23} \\ 0 & 0 & 1 \end{bmatrix}$$

A_{ij} represents the affine transformation of an image obtained by calculating linear homography of u_{i0}.

After detecting features in all the images, we need to match them to find their relative arrangements. For this, we match the overlapping features using the k-nearest neighbors (with k = 4) in the feature space to obtain overlapping features. This method is employed to take into consideration the fact that each feature may overlap in more than one image.

Image matching

By now, we have obtained the features and have the matches between features. Now we need to obtain the matching images to form the panorama. To form a panorama, we need a small number of images to match any image, so as to find adjacent images. The algorithm suggests the use of six matching images to the current image. This section is performed in two parts. First, we estimate the homography with which the two frames are compatible and we find a set of inliers for the same. For this, we use the RANSAC algorithm. Then we use a probabilistic model to verify the match between the images.

Homography estimation using RANSAC

The RANSAC algorithm, short for Random Sample Consensus, is an algorithm that uses a small set of randomly chosen matches in images to estimate the image transformation parameters. For image stitching, we use four feature matches to compute the homography between them. For this, the algorithm proposes the use of the direct linear transformation method described by R. Hartley and A. Zisserman. This is performed for 500 iterations and ultimately, the solution with the maximum number of *inliers* is chosen. Inliers are those features whose linear projections are consistent with the homography, H, up to a specified tolerance value for pixels. By performing probability calculations, it was found that the probability of finding a match is very high. For example, if inliers between images match with a probability of 0.5, the probability of not finding the homography is $1 * 10^{-14}$. Hence, RANSAC is quite successful at estimating H. This method is called the maximum likelihood estimation.

Verification of image matches using a probabilistic model

By the model obtained till now, we have a set of feature matches within the overlap region (inliers), and some features within the area of overlap that do not match (outliers). Using a probabilistic model, we will verify that the obtained set of inliers and outliers produces a valid image match. The algorithm makes the assumption that the probability of the ith feature matching is an independent Bernoulli trial. The two equations that are obtained from this are shown as follows:

$$p\left(f^{1:n_f} \mid m = 1\right) = B\left(n_i; n_f, p_1\right)$$

$$p\left(f^{1:n_f} \mid m = 0\right) = B\left(n_i; n_f, p_0\right)$$

Here, n_f represents the total number of features present in the overlap area. n_i represents the total number of inliers. m specifies whether the two images have been matched correctly or not. P_1 is the probability of the feature being an inlier, given a correct image match. P_0 is the probability that the feature is not an inlier, given a correct image match. $f^{1:n_f}$ represents the set of feature matches $\left\{ f^{(i)} \mid i \in \{1,2,3,\ldots,n_f\} \right\}$. B represents the binomial distribution, as shown here:

$$B(x;n,p) = \frac{n!}{x!(n-x)!} p^x (1-p)^{n-x}$$

For the purpose of this algorithm, the values of P_1 and P_2 are set to 0.6 and 0.1, respectively. Using Bayes rule, we can calculate the probability of an image match being valid as:

$$p\left(m=1 \mid f^{1:n_f}\right) = \frac{p\left(f^{1:n_f} \mid m=1\right) p(m=1)}{p\left(f^{1:n_f}\right)}$$

An image match is considered to be valid if the value of the preceding expression is greater than a pre-chosen minimum probability. The algorithm suggests the use of $p_{min} = 0.999$ and $p(m=1) = 10^{-6}$. The match is accepted if the following equation is satisfied, and rejected otherwise:

$$\frac{B(n_i;n_f,p_1)p(m=1)}{B(n_i;n_f,p_0)p(m=0)} > \frac{p_{min}}{1-p_{min}}$$

A condition that arises from the assumption made earlier is that for a valid image match the following equation must be satisfied:

$$n_i > 8 + 0.3n_f$$

In the original paper, the authors also proposed a method by which the parameters can be learnt from the images rather than assigning fixed values to them.

Bundle adjustment

Brown and Lowe's algorithm proposes the use of bundle adjustment to obtain all the camera parameters, jointly for a given set of matches between the images. For this, images are added to a bundle adjuster in decreasing order of the number of feature matches. Each time, the new image is initialized with the rotation and focal length of the image to which it matched. Then we use the Levenberg-Marquadt algorithm to update the camera parameters. The Levenberg-Marquadt algorithm is generally used to solve non-linear least squares problems in curve fitting problems.

This algorithm tries to minimize the sum of the squared projection errors. For this, each feature is projected on to every other image to which the original image matches, and then the sum of the squared distances is minimized with respect to the camera parameters. If the kth feature in one image matches the 1th feature in another, we obtain the residual for the projection as follows:

$$r_{ij}^k = u_i^k - p_{ij}^k$$

Here, u_i^k represents the kth feature in the ith image, r_{ij}^k is the residual after the projection of the kth feature from j^{th} image on the ith image, and p_{ij}^k is the projection of u_{ij}^k from the jth image on the ith image.

Then, the error function is calculated by summing up all the robustified residual field errors, over all the features, spanning all the images. For this robustification, the Huber robust error function is used:

$$h(x) = \begin{cases} |x|^2 & ; if \ |x| < \sigma \\ 2\sigma|x| - \sigma^2 & ; otherwise \end{cases}$$

On solving this, we get a non-linear equation, which is solved using the Levenberg-Marquadt algorithm, to estimate the values of the camera parameters.

Automatic panoramic straightening

So far, the algorithm has been able to successfully find matches between images and able to stitch them together. However, there still exists an unknown 3D rotation component, which causes the panorama to be formed in a wave-like output, as shown in the following figure:

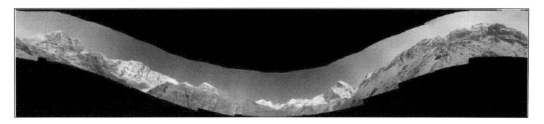

This arises mainly due to the fact that the camera would not have been perfectly level while clicking the multiple images.

This is solved by taking a heuristic into consideration regarding the way people click panoramic images. It is assumed that it is highly unlikely for a user to rotate the camera while clicking the image, so the camera vectors generally lie on the same plane. So, we try to find the null vector of the covariance matrix of the camera vectors and the vector normal to the plane of the center and horizon. This way, we can then apply the rotation on the images to effectively remove the wavy effect.

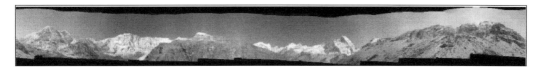

Gain compensation

Gain is the camera parameter that describes the sensitivity of the image to light. Different images could have been clicked at different levels of gain. To overcome this situation, we make use of gain compensation, as shown here:

Gain compensation refers to the normalization of the gain in images to facilitate a seamlessly stitched image. The method used is similar to the one used to compute the camera parameters. The error function used here is the sum of the errors in gain-normalized intensities for all the overlapping pixels:

Multi-band blending

Even after gain compensation, the stitching doesn't appear to be seamless. We need to apply a good blending algorithm to join the images without it being noticeable that the image has been stitched from multiple images.

For this, we apply a good blending strategy. We choose a blending algorithm in which we assign a weight function to each image. This weight function varies linearly with weight = 1 at the center and weight = 0 at the edges. This weight function is also extended to a spherical coordinate system. A simple weighted sum of the intensities along each ray can be calculated using these weight functions, but this would cause high frequency areas to be blurred out.

Due to this, we need to implement multi-band blending. The multi-band blending blends low frequency regions over a large area, where it blends high frequency regions over a relatively smaller area. We assign weights to each image, using $W_{max}^i(\theta,\phi)$, such that the value of $W_{max}^i(\theta,\phi)$ is 1 where there is maximum weight in the image and 0 where the maximum weight for the region is from some other image. We then successively blur out these weight graphs to ultimately get the blending weights for each band.

Then we linearly combine the overlapping images for each band with respect to the blend weights. The amount of blurring depends on the frequency of the band. This results in the high frequency bands being blended over short regions, while the low frequency bands get blended over large regions:

Image stitching using OpenCV

The following is the image stitching pipeline:

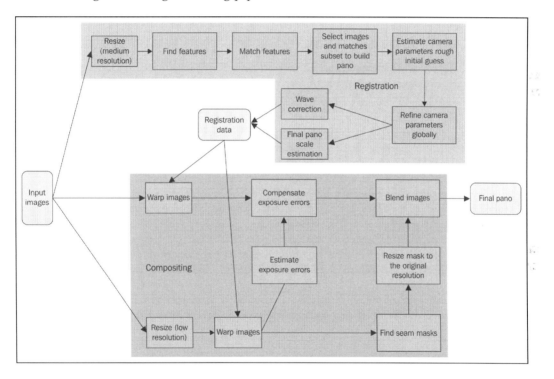

We will now see how to implement image stitching.

First, we will set up our project in the same way as we did for all the previous chapters. We will use the package name `com.packtpub.masteringopencvandroid.chapter6` for this project. First, we will edit our manifest file.

We will add all the required permissions to this project. We require the permissions to access the camera, and also to read and write to the external storage. So, add the following code to your manifest:

```
<uses-permission android:name="android.permission.CAMERA" />
<uses-permission
    android:name="android.permission.WRITE_EXTERNAL_STORAGE" />
<uses-permission
    android:name="android.permission.READ_PHONE_STATE" />
<uses-permission
    android:name="android.permission.READ_EXTERNAL_STORAGE" />
```

Then we will declare our activities. We only require one activity for this project. We will call it the `StitchingActivity`.

Setting up Android NDK

We require NDK for this project as the stitching module is unavailable in OpenCV's Java SDK. So, we will write the C++ code and compile it using Android NDK in order for it to be used as a part of our project. To do this, first download NDK from `http://developer.android.com/tools/sdk/ndk` and extract it to a location on your computer. Then go to your `local.properties` file and add the following line:

```
ndk.dir=<location of the ndk directory>
```

Next, go to your `build.gradle` file that is located in the main module of your project. In this file, inside the `defaultConfig` tag, add the following code:

```
ndk {
    moduleName "stitcher"
}
```

This is the name of the module, which will contain our functions, where our computations will be performed. Now, under the `android` tag, after `defaultConfig` ends, add the following lines:

```
sourceSets.main {
    jniLibs.srcDir 'src/main/libs'
    jni.srcDirs = [] //disable automatic ndk-build call
}
```

This defines where our compiled libraries will be located. After this, we need to set up the NDK part of our project. In the `src` folder, add a folder called `jni`. In this folder, we need to create two files. The first one is `Android.mk`. This contains information about the files in the project. Copy the following lines to this file. Remember to replace `OpenCV4AndroidSDK` with the location on your computer:

```
LOCAL_PATH := $(call my-dir)

include $(CLEAR_VARS)

OPENCV_CAMERA_MODULES:=on
OPENCV_INSTALL_MODULES:=on

include <OpenCV4AndroidSDK>/sdk/native/jni/OpenCV.mk

LOCAL_MODULE    := stitcher
LOCAL_SRC_FILES := stitcher.cpp
LOCAL_LDLIBS += -llog -ldl

include $(BUILD_SHARED_LIBRARY)
```

Now, create another file named `Application.mk`. This defines the architectures for which the code has to be compiled. Copy the following lines to this file:

```
APP_STL := gnustl_static
APP_CPPFLAGS := -frtti -fexceptions
APP_ABI := armeabi-v7a
APP_PLATFORM := android-8
```

Now we are all set to use NDK code in our project.

The layout and Java code

Next we will draw our layout. For this project, we only need one layout with one `ImageView` tag to display the stitched image and two `Buttons`. One of the buttons is used to click more images and one is used to signify that there are no more images to be clicked. We will also put all the items in a `ScrollView` tag to be able to see the full image if its size exceeds the screen size. Our `activity_stitching.xml` file is as follows:

```
<?xml version="1.0" encoding="utf-8"?>
<ScrollView xmlns:android=
  "http://schemas.android.com/apk/res/android"
    android:layout_width="match_parent"
    android:layout_height="match_parent" >
```

```
<LinearLayout android:orientation="vertical"
  android:layout_width="match_parent"
    android:layout_height="wrap_content">

    <ImageView
        android:layout_width="match_parent"
        android:layout_height="0dp"
        android:layout_weight="0.5"
        android:id="@+id/ivImage" />
    <LinearLayout
        android:layout_width="match_parent"
        android:layout_height="wrap_content"
        android:orientation="horizontal">
        <Button
            android:layout_width="match_parent"
            android:layout_height="wrap_content"
            android:layout_weight="0.5"
            android:id="@+id/bClickImage"
            android:text="Click more images"/>
        <Button
            android:layout_width="match_parent"
            android:layout_height="wrap_content"
            android:layout_weight="0.5"
            android:id="@+id/bDone"
            android:text="Done"/>
    </LinearLayout>

</LinearLayout>
</ScrollView>
```

Now we have to write our Java code. In the `StitchingActivity.java` file, in your OpenCV `BaseLoaderCallback` object, edit the `onManagerConnected` function by adding the following line in case `LoaderCallbackInterface.SUCCESS`:

```
System.loadLibrary("stitcher");
```

Notice that this is the same name that we gave our module in our `Android.mk` file. In our Java code, we will first declare and initialize all the variables that we will need. We have a button called `bClickImage`, which, on clicking, calls Android's camera intent and requests the system's camera app to click a picture and sends it to the app. We will convert this `Bitmap` image into an OpenCV `Mat` and store it in an `ArrayList`. We will stitch all the images together in the end, when the user clicks on the `bDone` button. The `onClickListener` for both the buttons is as follows:

```
bClickImage.setOnClickListener(new View.OnClickListener() {
    @Override
    public void onClick(View v) {
```

```
            Intent intent = new
              Intent(MediaStore.ACTION_IMAGE_CAPTURE);
            File imagesFolder = new File(FILE_LOCATION);
            imagesFolder.mkdirs();
            File image = new File(imagesFolder, "panorama_"+
              (clickedImages.size()+1) + ".jpg");
            fileUri = Uri.fromFile(image);
            Log.d("StitchingActivity", "File URI = " +
              fileUri.toString());
            intent.putExtra(MediaStore.EXTRA_OUTPUT, fileUri);
              // set the image file name

            // start the image capture Intent
            startActivityForResult(intent, CLICK_PHOTO);
        }
    });

    bDone.setOnClickListener(new View.OnClickListener() {
        @Override
        public void onClick(View v) {
            if(clickedImages.size()==0){
                Toast.makeText(getApplicationContext(),
                  "No images clicked", Toast.LENGTH_SHORT).show();
            } else if(clickedImages.size()==1){
                Toast.makeText(getApplicationContext(), "Only one
                  image clicked", Toast.LENGTH_SHORT).show();
                Bitmap image = Bitmap.createBitmap(src.cols(),
                  src.rows(), Bitmap.Config.ARGB_8888);
                Utils.matToBitmap(src, image);
                ivImage.setImageBitmap(image);
            } else {
                createPanorama();
            }
        }
    });
```

The onActivityResult function is called when the camera intent returns from the camera app. We need to check whether an image has been clicked and add it to the ArrayList, if required. We will use OpenCV's BitmapToMat function to convert the image from an Android Bitmap to an OpenCV Mat. The code is as follows:

```
switch(requestCode) {
    case CLICK_PHOTO:
        if(resultCode == RESULT_OK){
            try {
```

```
            final InputStream imageStream =
              getContentResolver().openInputStream(fileUri);
            final Bitmap selectedImage =
              BitmapFactory.decodeStream(imageStream);
            src = new Mat(selectedImage.getHeight(),
              selectedImage.getWidth(), CvType.CV_8UC4);
            Imgproc.resize(src, src, new Size(src.rows()/4,
              src.cols()/4));
            Utils.bitmapToMat(selectedImage, src);
            Imgproc.cvtColor(src, src, Imgproc.COLOR_BGR2RGB);
            clickedImages.add(src);
        } catch (FileNotFoundException e) {
            e.printStackTrace();
        }
    }
    break;
}
```

In `onClickListener` for bDone, we called a `createPanorama` function. In this function, we will execute an `AsyncTask`, as this is a computationally intensive task. In `AsyncTask`, we will call upon our NDK to perform the actual computation. This is what our `doInBackground` looks like:

```
Mat srcRes = new Mat();
int success = StitchPanorama(clickedImages.toArray(),
  clickedImages.size(), srcRes.getNativeObjAddr());
if(success==0){
    return null;
}
Imgproc.cvtColor(srcRes, srcRes, Imgproc.Color_BGR2RGBA);
Bitmap bitmap = Bitmap.createBitmap(srcRes.cols(), srcRes.rows(),
  Bitmap.Config.ARGB_8888);
Utils.matToBitmap(srcRes, bitmap);
return bitmap;
```

We also need to declare the `StitchPanorama` function as a native function so that Android knows where to look for it when executing:

```
public native int StitchPanorama(Object images[],
  int size, long addrSrcRes);
```

After this, in `onPostExecute`, we just need to set the returned `Bitmap` as the source for `ImageView`. This completes our Java code for this project, and all the major stitching is done using the C++ code.

The C++ code

In your `jni` folder, create the `stitcher.cpp` file. Notice that this is the same name as set in the `Android.mk` file. First, we need to include some libraries that we will require. We will also declare some namespaces that we will be using and some global variables as follows:

```
#include <jni.h>
#include <vector>

#include "opencv2/imgproc/imgproc.hpp"
#include "opencv2/highgui/highgui.hpp"
#include <opencv2/stitching/stitcher.hpp>
using namespace cv;
using namespace std;

char FILEPATH[100] = "/storage/emulated/0/Download/PacktBook/
  Chapter6/panorama_stitched.jpg";
```

Then we need to declare our function and write our code in it. To declare the function, write the following code:

```
extern "C" {
    JNIEXPORT jint JNICALL Java_com_packtpub_
      masteringopencvandroid_chapter6_StitchingActivity_
      StitchPanorama(JNIEnv*, jobject, jobjectArray, jint, jlong);
    JNIEXPORT jint JNICALL Java_com_packtpub_
      masteringopencvandroid_chapter6_StitchingActivity_
      StitchPanorama(JNIEnv* env, jobject, jobjectArray
      images, jint size, jlong resultMatAddr)
    {
        ...
    }
}
```

The ellipses are placeholders for where our code will go. Notice the variables and their orders compared to the variables declared in our Java code. First, we will initialize some variables and also convert the Mat object that we sent from Java to a C++ Mat:

```
jint resultReturn = 0;
vector<Mat> clickedImages = vector<Mat>();
Mat output_stitched = Mat();
Mat& srcRes = *(Mat*)resultMatAddr, img;
```

Here, we have used the address of the Mat object and type-casted it to a C++ Mat pointer. Next we need to convert the Mat array sent from Java to a C++ vector. We will use the following code:

```
jclass clazz = (env)->FindClass("org/opencv/core/Mat");
jmethodID getNativeObjAddr = (env)->GetMethodID(clazz,
  "getNativeObjAddr", "()J");

for(int i=0; i < size; i++){
    jobject obj = (env->GetObjectArrayElement(images, i));
    jlong result = (env)->CallLongMethod(obj,
      getNativeObjAddr, NULL);
    img = *(Mat*)result;
    resize(img, img, Size(img.rows/10, img.cols/10));
    clickedImages.push_back(img);
    env->DeleteLocalRef(obj);
}
env->DeleteLocalRef(images);
```

We need to manually delete the local objects as the C++ code doesn't automatically call the garbage collector, and being on mobile, it is highly important to optimize the memory use.

Now we will use OpenCV's stitcher module to stitch our images:

```
Stitcher stitcher = Stitcher::createDefault();
Stitcher::Status status = stitcher.stitch(clickedImages,
  output_stitched);

output_stitched.copyTo(srcRes);

imwrite(FILEPATH, srcRes);

if (status == Stitcher::OK)
    resultReturn = 1;
else
    resultReturn = 0;

return resultReturn;
```

We have used the default setup for stitching the images; however, the stitcher module allows the modification of the pipeline by giving more control to the developer. Check out the available options at `http://docs.opencv.org/modules/stitching/doc/introduction.html`.

Now we just need to build our C++ code file to generate the object files that our Java code will use to make function calls to C++ functions. For this, you will need to open the terminal/command prompt, and then use the `cd` command to change the active directory to `<project_dir>/app/src/main/jni`. Now we need to build our files. For this, you need to use the following command:

```
<ndk_dir>/ndk-build
```

This will generate our object files and place them in the `obj` and `libs` folders.

This completes our project on image stitching using OpenCV on Android. You can see the stitched results in the following images.

The following is the first sample image:

The following is the second sample image:

The following is the result of applying image stitching over these two sample images:

There are chances that your code might crash due to the high memory requirements of the stitcher module. This is a limitation of the mobile ecosystem and can be overcome by including a server in the middle to perform the computations instead. You can modify the source of the app to send the images to the server, which in turn performs the stitching and returns the stitched result, which can be displayed in the app.

Summary

In this chapter, we saw how panoramic images are stitched. We took a look at image alignment by finding homography, using RANSAC, and image stitching as a whole. We also saw how it can be implemented in Android using OpenCV. These image alignment techniques can also be used for video stabilization. In the next chapter, we will take a look at how we can make use of machine learning algorithms to automate some of the complex tasks that generally require a human to be present.

7
Bringing Your Apps to Life with OpenCV Machine Learning

With so much data around us, we need better systems and applications to process it and extract relevant information out of it. A field of computer science that deals with this is **machine learning**. In this chapter, we will take a look at the different machine learning techniques that can be used to exploit all the data around us and build smart applications that can deal with unencountered situations or scenarios, without any form of human intervention.

In the recent years, computer vision and machine learning have formed a strong synergy between them, thus enabling technologies that have helped build some extremely efficient and useful applications. Humanoids, robotic arms, and assembly lines are some of the examples where computer vision and machine learning find applications. Developers and researchers are now trying to exploit mobile platforms and build light-weight applications that can be used by common people. In the following section, we will build an application for **Optical Character Recognition (OCR)** using standard OpenCV and Android APIs. Toward the end, we will revisit the Sudoku solving application that we started developing in *Chapter 2, Detecting Basic Features in Images*.

We will understand the machine learning techniques alongside building applications.

Optical Character Recognition

Optical Character Recognition (**OCR**) is one of the favorite topics of research in computer vision and machine learning. There are a lot of efficient off-the-shelf implementations and algorithms readily available for OCR, but for better understanding of the concepts, we will build our own OCR Android application. Before we get down to writing the code for our application, let's take some time to take a look at the different character recognition techniques and how they work. In this chapter, we will use two standard machine learning techniques: **k-nearest neighbors** (**KNN**) and **Support Vector Machines** (**SVM**), while building our applications.

The aim of this chapter is to build a real-time digit recognition application. The application will have a live camera output being displayed on the mobile screen and as soon as the camera captures a digit, we will recognize the digit.

OCR using k-nearest neighbors

k-nearest neighbors is the one of the simplest algorithms used for supervised classification. In KNN, we give the training dataset and their corresponding labels as input. An n-dimensional space is created (where n is the length of each training data) and every training data is plotted as a point in it. While classification, we plot the data to be classified in the same n-dimensional space, and calculate the distance of that point from every other point in the space. The distance computed is used to find an appropriate class for the testing data.

Here is a step–by-step explanation of the working of the algorithm:

1. Choose a user-defined value of k.
2. Store the training data along with their classes in the form of a row vector.
3. Take the input query (data to be classified) and calculate the distance from it to every other row vector in the training data (meaning of distance is explained in the following box).
4. Sort all the row vectors in the ascending order of their distance (calculated in the previous step) from the query data.
5. Finally, from the first k sorted row vectors, choose the class (training labels), which has the majority of row vectors as the predicted class.

Distance between vectors

In Euclidean Space, we define the distance between two vectors as:

$$\left(\sum_{i=1}^{n}\left|x_i - y_i\right|^2\right)^{1/2}$$

where, x_i and y_i are the ith dimension values of the two vectors x and y respectively. n is the length of the training vectors (x and y in our case). The algorithm does not put any restriction on the type of distance we can use. Some other types of distances that we can use are **Manhattan distance**, Maximum distance and the likes. Refer to http://en.wikipedia.org/wiki/Distance for some other definitions of distance.

Simple enough! How do we use it with image data? For us to be able to use KNN on the image data, we need to convert the training images to some sort of a row vector.

Consider a 10x10 grayscale image of any digit from one to nine. The easiest and the fastest way to get a feature vector from the 10x10 image is to convert it into a 1x100 row vector. This can be done by appending the rows in the image one after another. This way, we can convert all the images in our training set to row vectors for later use in the KNN classifier.

To make it easier for us to build the digit recognition application, we will break it down into smaller parts listed as follows and finally use them together:

- Making a camera application
- Handling the training data
- Recognizing the captured digit

Making a camera application

We will begin by building a simple camera application that displays the camera output on the screen, as we did in *Chapter 4, Drilling Deeper into Object Detection – Using Cascade Classifiers*:

- Create a new Android project in Eclipse (or Android Studio)
- Initialize OpenCV in the project (refer to *Chapter 1, Applying Effects to Images*).

- Add `JavaCameraView` to the main activity using the following code snippet:

```
<org.opencv.android.JavaCameraView
        android:layout_width="fill_parent"
        android:layout_height="fill_parent"
        android:visibility="gone"
        android:id="@+id/java_surface_view"
        opencv:camera_id="any" />
```

Once the camera is in place, draw a square on the screen that will help the user to localize the digit that he/she wants to recognize. The user will point to the digit and try to bring it within the square drawn on the screen (as shown in Figure 1). Copy the following piece of code in the Mat `onCameraFrame()` function:

```
Mat temp = inputFrame.rgba();

Core.rectangle(temp, new Point(temp.cols()/2 - 200,
    temp.rows() / 2 - 200), new Point(temp.cols() / 2 + 200,
    temp.rows() / 2 + 200), new Scalar(255,255,255),1);
```

In this code, we take the size of the frame captured by the mobile camera and draw a 400x400 (can vary according to the screen size) white rectangle in the center of the image (as shown in Figure 1). That's it. The camera application is ready. Next, is handling the training data in the application.

Figure 1. Screenshot of the camera application

Handling the training data

This is the trickiest part of the application. Training data plays a crucial role in any machine learning application. The amount of data that such applications deal with is usually in the order of few megabytes. This may not be a concern for a normal desktop application, but for a mobile application (because of resource constraints), even handling around 50 megabytes can lead to performance issues, if not done properly. The code needs to be concise, to the point, and should have minimum memory leaks.

For this application, we will make use of a publically available handwritten digits dataset — MNIST, to train the KNN classifier.

> The MNIST database (`http://yann.lecun.com/exdb/mnist/`) of handwritten digits available from this page, has a training set of 60,000 examples and a test set of 10,000 examples. It is a subset of a larger set available from MNIST. The digits have been size-normalized and centered in a fixed-size image. (Text taken from Prof. Yann LeCun's web page, which is available at `http://yann.lecun.com`.)

First, download the MNIST training data using the following links:

- Training images at `http://yann.lecun.com/exdb/mnist/train-images-idx3-ubyte.gz`

- Training labels at `http://yann.lecun.com/exdb/mnist/train-labels-idx1-ubyte.gz`

Extract the downloaded files and transfer them to an Android phone (make sure you have around 60 MB of free space available).

Getting back to our application, create a new `DigitRecognizer` class that will handle all the tasks related to digit recognition, including loading the dataset into the application, training the classifier, and finally, recognizing the digit. Add a new Java class to the project and name it `DigitRecognizer`.

So, we already have the training images and training labels stored in the phone. We need to load the data into the application. For this, all we have to do is read the data from these files and make them compatible with OpenCV's API.

Add a new function void `ReadMNISTData()` to the `DigitRecognizer` class created earlier. This function will read the MNIST dataset and store it in the form of a Mat (OpenCV's class to store images). Read the dataset in two parts: first, the training images and then the training labels.

In `ReadMNISTData()`, create a new `File` object that will store the path to the phone's SD card (as shown in the following code). In case the file is in the phone's internal memory, skip this step and provide an absolute path of the file that we wish to use later in the code:

```
File external_storage = Environment.getExternalStorageDirectory();
```

After doing this, create another `File` object that will point to the exact file that we want to read in our application, and an `InputStreamReader` object that will help us in reading the file:

```
File mnist_images_file = new File(external_storage, images_path);

FileInputStream images_reader = new
    FileInputStream(mnist_images_file);
```

Here, `images_path` is the absolute path of the `train-images-idx3-ubyte.idx3` training images file.

Before we continue with the code, we need to understand how images are stored in the file. Here is the description of the contents of the training images file:

```
[offset]  [type]           [value]           [description]
0000      32 bit integer   0x00000803(2051)  magic number
0004      32 bit integer   60000             number of images
0008      32 bit integer   28                number of rows
0012      32 bit integer   28                number of columns
0016      unsigned byte    ??                pixel
0017      unsigned byte    ??                pixel
........
xxxx      unsigned byte    ??                pixel
```

Pixels are organized row-wise. Pixel values are 0 to 255, where 0 represents the background (white) and 255 represents the foreground (black).

With this information, we can continue writing the code:

```
Mat training_images = null;

try{
        //Read the file headers which contain the
          total number of images and dimensions.
          First 16 bytes hold the header
        /*
```

```
byte 0 -3 : Magic Number (Not to be used)
byte 4 - 7: Total number of images in the dataset
byte 8 - 11: width of each image in the dataset
byte 12 - 15: height of each image in the dataset
*/

byte [] header = new byte[16];
images_reader.read(header, 0, 16);

//Combining the bytes to form an integer
ByteBuffer temp = ByteBuffer.wrap(header, 4, 12);
total_images = temp.getInt();
width = temp.getInt();
height = temp.getInt();

//Total number of pixels in each image
int px_count = width * height;
training_images = new Mat(total_images, px_count,
    CvType.CV_8U);

//images_data = new byte[total_images][px_count];
//Read each image and store it in an array.

for (int i = 0 ; i < total_images ; i++)
{
    byte[] image = new byte[px_count];
    images_reader.read(image, 0, px_count);
    training_images.put(i,0,image);
}
training_images.convertTo(training_images,
    CvType.CV_32FC1);
images_reader.close();
}
catch (IOException e)
{
    Log.i("MNIST Read Error:", "" + e.getMessage());
}
```

In the preceding code, first, we read the first 16 bytes of the file, which stores the number of images, height, and width of the images (refer to the aforementioned table describing the contents of the file). Using the `ByteBuffer` class, we get four integers from the 16 bytes by combining four bytes, one each for an integer.

In OpenCV, KNN's implementation requires us to pass all the feature vectors using the Mat class. Every training image needs to be converted to a row vector that will form one row of the Mat object, which will be passed to the KNN classifier. For example, if we have 5,000 training images each with dimensions 20x20, we will need a Mat object with dimensions 5000x400 that can be passed to OpenCV's KNN training function. Confused? Continue reading!

Take a 20x20 image from the training dataset and convert it to a 1x400 vector by appending rows one after another. Do this for all the images. At the end, we will have 5,000 such 1x400 vectors. Now, create a new Mat object with dimensions 5000x400, and each row of this new Mat object will be the 1x400 vector that we got just now by resizing the original images in the dataset.

This is what the preceding piece of code intends to do. First, read all the pixels in an image using the following code:

```
byte[] image = new byte[px_count];
images_reader.read(image, 0, px_count);
```

Here, px_count is the total number of pixels in a training image and image is a row vector that stores the image. As explained earlier, we need to copy these row vectors to a Mat object (training_images refers to the Mat object that will be used to store these training images). Copy the image row vector to training_images, as follows:

```
training_images.put(i,0,image);
```

Training data is in place. We now need their corresponding labels. As we did for training images, their corresponding labels (label values are from 0 to 9) can be read in the same way. The contents of the labels file are arranged in the following way:

```
[offset] [type]          [value]           [description]
0000     32 bit integer  0x00000801(2049)  magic
  number (MSB first)
0004     32 bit integer  60000             number of items
0008     unsigned byte   ??                label
0009     unsigned byte   ??                label
........
xxxx     unsigned byte   ??                label
```

Here is the code to read the labels:

```
//Read Labels
        Mat training_labels = null;

        labels_data = new byte[total_images];
```

```
File mnist_labels_file = new File(external_storage,
  labels_path);
FileInputStream labels_reader = new
  FileInputStream(mnist_labels_file);

try{

    training_labels = new Mat(total_images, 1,
      CvType.CV_8U);
    Mat temp_labels = new Mat(1, total_images,
      CvType.CV_8U);
    byte[] header = new byte[8];
    //Read the header
    labels_reader.read(header, 0, 8);
    //Read all the labels at once
    labels_reader.read(labels_data,0,total_images);
    temp_labels.put(0,0, labels_data);

    //Take a transpose of the image
    Core.transpose(temp_labels, training_labels);
    training_labels.convertTo(training_labels,
      CvType.CV_32FC1);
    labels_reader.close();
}
catch (IOException e)
{
    Log.i("MNIST Read Error:", "" + e.getMessage());
}
```

The basis of the preceding code is similar to the code used for reading images.

We have successfully loaded the training data in our application. At this point, you can use some diagnostic tools of Android to check the memory usage of the application. An important point that you need to take care of is to not duplicate the data. Doing this will increase the amount of memory consumed, which can affect the performance of your application as well as other applications running on your phone. Pass the `training_images` and `training_labels` Mat objects to OpenCV's KNN classifier object:

```
knn = new CvKNearest();
knn.train(training_images, training_labels, new Mat(),
  false, 10, false);
```

The KNN classifier is ready. We are now ready to classify the data.

Recognizing digits

This is the final part of the application. Here, we use the frames that are captured from the camera as an input to the classifier and allow the classifier to predict the digit in the frame.

To begin with, add a new function void `FindMatch()` to the `DigitRecognizer` class created in the previous section as follows:

```
void FindMatch(Mat test_image)
    {

        //Dilate the image
        Imgproc.dilate(test_image, test_image,
          Imgproc.getStructuringElement(Imgproc.CV_SHAPE_CROSS,
          new Size(3,3)));
        //Resize the image to match it with the sample image size
        Imgproc.resize(test_image, test_image, new
          Size(width, height));
        //Convert the image to grayscale
        Imgproc.cvtColor(test_image, test_image,
          Imgproc.COLOR_RGB2GRAY);
        //Adaptive Threshold
        Imgproc.adaptiveThreshold(test_image,test_image,
          255,Imgproc.ADAPTIVE_THRESH_MEAN_C,
          Imgproc.THRESH_BINARY_INV,15, 2);

        Mat test = new Mat(1, test_image.rows() *
          test_image.cols(), CvType.CV_32FC1);
        int count = 0;
        for(int i = 0 ; i < test_image.rows(); i++)
        {
            for(int j = 0 ; j < test_image.cols(); j++) {
                test.put(0, count, test_image.get(i, j)[0]);
                count++;
            }
        }

        Mat results = new Mat(1, 1, CvType.CV_8U);

        knn.find_nearest(test, 10, results, new Mat(), new Mat());
        Log.i("Result:", "" + results.get(0,0)[0]);

    }
```

 Note: Images in the training dataset are 28x28 binary images.

The camera output is not directly usable. We need to preprocess the images to bring them as close as possible to the images in the training dataset for our classifier to give accurate results.

Perform the following steps (preferably in the same order) to make the camera output usable by the KNN classifier:

1. Dilate the image to make the digit more prominent in the image and reduce any background noise.

2. Resize the image to 28x28. The training images are also of this dimension.

3. Convert the image to a grayscale image.

4. Perform adaptive threshold on the image to get a binary image.

 All the parameters used in the code here are subject to lighting conditions. You are requested to tweak these parameters to suit their environment for best results.

After following these steps, we will have a test that needs to go into the KNN classifier that we trained in the previous section. Before this can happen, there is one more thing that needs to be done to the test image—transforming the image to a row vector (remember the transformations we did to training images?). Convert the 28x28 test image to a 1x784 row vector. Use the following piece of code to transform the image:

```
Mat test = new Mat(1, test_image.rows() * test_image.cols(), CvType.
CV_32FC1);
int count = 0;
for(int i = 0 ; i < test_image.rows(); i++)
{
    for(int j = 0 ; j < test_image.cols(); j++) {
        test.put(0, count, test_image.get(i, j)[0]);
        count++;
    }
}
```

Finally, pass the transformed `test` image to the KNN classifier and store the result in the 1x1 Mat object `results`. The last two parameters in the `find_nearest` function are optional:

```
knn.find_nearest(test, 10, results, new Mat(), new Mat());
```

One last thing, how and when do we call the `FindMatch` function? Since we are building a real-time digit recognition application, we need to perform the matching operation on every output frame of the camera. Because of this, we need to call this function in `onCameraFrame()` in the main activity class. The function should finally look like this:

```
public Mat onCameraFrame(CvCameraViewFrame inputFrame) {

        //Get image size and draw a rectangle on the image for
reference
        Mat temp = inputFrame.rgba();
        Core.rectangle(temp, new Point(temp.cols()/2 - 200, temp.
rows() / 2 - 200), new Point(temp.cols() / 2 + 200, temp.rows() / 2 +
200), new Scalar(255,255,255),1);
        Mat digit = temp.submat(temp.rows()/2 - 180, temp.rows() / 2 +
180, temp.cols() / 2 - 180, temp.cols() / 2 + 180).clone();
        Core.transpose(digit,digit);
        mnist.FindMatch(digit);

        return temp;
    }
```

We take the RGBA image of the camera output and extract the part of the image enclosed by the rectangle that we drew on the screen before. We want the user to bring the digit within the rectangle for it to be successfully recognized.

Since our application is written for landscape mode (set in the `AndroidManifest.xml` file) but we use it in the portrait mode, we need to transpose the test image before we can run the recognition algorithm. Hence, run this command:

```
Core.transpose(digit,digit);
```

We have successfully created a real-time digit recognition application. Let's take a look at another machine learning technique that can be used in recognizing digits.

OCR using Support Vector Machines

Support Vector Machines (SVMs) are supervised learning algorithms that are commonly used for classification and regression. In SVMs, the training data is divided into different regions using infinite hyperplanes, and each region represents a class. To test data, we plot the point in the same space as the training points and using the hyperplanes compute the region where the test point lies. SVMs are useful when dealing with high-dimensional data.

For details on SVMs, you can refer to `http://www.support-vector-machines.org/`.

In this section, we will learn how to use SVMs for digit recognition. As in KNN, to train an SVM, we will directly use the training images without any image manipulations or detecting any extra features.

 Instead of directly using the training images, it is possible to extract some features from the images and use those features as training data for the SVM. One of the OpenCV tutorials implemented in Python follows a different path. Here, they first deskew the image using affine transformations, then compute Histogram of Orientation Gradients. These HoG features are used to train the SVM. The reason why we are not following the same path is because of the cost of computation involved in computing affine transformations and HoG.

Only slight modifications are involved in using SVM instead of KNN in the application that we built in the previous section. The basic camera application and handling training data remains as is. The only modification that has to happen is in the digit recognition part where we train the classifier.

In `ReadMNISTData()` function, instead of creating a KNN classifier object, we will create an SVM object. Remove the following lines where we declared and initialized a KNN object:

```
knn = new CvKNearest();
knn.train(training_images, training_labels,
   new Mat(), false, 10, false);
```

Now, replace them with the following lines (declaring and initializing an SVM object):

```
svm = new CvSVM();
svm.train(training_images, training_labels);
```

The SVM classifier is now ready. The next step for the KNN classifier is to pass a test image to the classifier and check the result. For this, we need to modify the `FindMatch()` function. Replace the line that uses KNN for classification with an appropriate line which uses SVM.

An optimization that the users can incorporate in the preceding application is that they can save the trained classifier in a file on the device. This will save time in training the classifier again and again.

Let's take a look at the following command:

```
knn.find_nearest(test, 10, results, new Mat(), new Mat());
```

We need to replace the preceding command with the following command:

```
svm.predict(test);
```

That's all. Our application is ready. We can run the application, check for the results, and probably compare which algorithm runs better under what condition.

Solving a Sudoku puzzle

Remember the Sudoku puzzle project in *Chapter 2, Detecting Basic Features in Images*? Now is the perfect time to revisit this project and see whether we can use anything that we learnt in this chapter to complete this application. So, in *Chapter 2, Detecting Basic Features in Images*, we had successfully detected the Sudoku puzzle. Only two things were left in that application: recognizing digits and solving the Sudoku puzzle.

Recognizing digits in the puzzle

Let's pick up from where we left in *Chapter 2, Detecting Basic Features in Images*. After detecting the grid successfully, we need to further break down the grid into 81 small squares. There are many possible ways of doing this, but here, we will look at only three techniques.

First, the easiest of all is to draw nine equally spaced vertical and horizontal lines each on the image, and assume the digits to be placed within the boxes made by these lines.

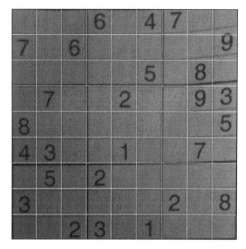

Figure 2. Vertical and horizontal lines drawn on a Sudoku grid

The second way is using Hough lines. Apply Hough lines on the Sudoku grid and store all the lines that are returned. Ideally, nine vertical and nine horizontal lines should be returned but chances of this happening are very bleak, unless you have a very good camera and perfect lighting conditions. There will be missing or incomplete lines that will reduce the application's performance or may lead to false results.

The third way is using corner detection. Run any corner detection algorithm and get all the corners in the image. These corners represent the vertices of the boxes enclosing the digits. Once you have all the corners, you can join four corners to form a box and extract that part of the image.

The previously mentioned techniques may not always guarantee perfect results. Different techniques may perform better, depending on the surroundings and the kind of camera being used.

Extract all 89 images using any of the previously mentioned technique, and pass them through a pretrained digit classifier—SVM or KNN (as seen in the previous sections). Done! Take the output of the classifier and make a 9x9 integer matrix in your code, and fill it up with the corresponding digits recognized from the grid. So now we have the grid with us. Use any brute force or Artificial Intelligence algorithm to get the correct solution of the Sudoku puzzle. Different algorithms that can be used are as follows:

- Backtracking
- Genetic algorithms
- Sudoku as a constraint problem

Refer to `http://en.wikipedia.org/wiki/Sudoku_solving_algorithms` for a detailed explanation on these algorithms.

Summary

In this chapter, we looked at how to make an application intelligent by incorporating machine learning into them. We looked at Support Vector Machines and KNNs, and how we can use them to build applications that can learn patterns in user entered data. Till now we have covered many computer vision algorithms and their implementations in detail. In the next chapter, we will take a look at some commonly faced errors while building such applications, and some best practices that will help you make the applications more efficient.

8
Troubleshooting and Best Practices

Errors are an inevitable part of the development cycle—be it a website or a mobile application. Sometimes they are logical, syntactical, or even careless mistakes. Spending a lot of time on debugging or correcting errors can distract you and affect your productivity significantly. In this chapter, we will discuss some common errors that developers face while building applications. This can significantly reduce the time spent on debugging your code. Also, it is very important to build applications that are efficient. The second half of this chapter will deal with a few guidelines that can increase the performance of your applications.

Troubleshooting errors

This section talks about different possible errors that developers face while building an Android application, such as permission errors, and how to use **Logcat** to debug the code.

Permission errors

Every application in the Android ecosystem needs the user's permission to perform any critical operations involving user data, such as using the Internet or the camera, just to name a few. To ensure this, the application developers (in this case, us) have to request the user for permissions to perform any critical operations. Developers do this at the time of building the application by declaring all the required permissions in the Android project (more details on this will be explained in the following pages). While installing an application from the Play Store or otherwise, the user is prompted to grant or deny the permissions that the application requires.

Only when the user has granted all the permissions, the application can be installed on the mobile. This way, the user is aware of all the tasks, services, and features, such as using the Internet or storing data on your phone's memory, that the application is going to use.

How does Android ensure that all the necessary permissions have been granted? It is very likely that a developer might forget to declare a few permissions while building the application. To handle this, Android has a set of predefined tasks that require user permission before they can be performed. While generating the APK for the application, the code is checked for all such tasks and whether the corresponding permission has been declared by the developer. Once the code passes this test, a working APK is generated, which can be used to install the application on any Android phone. Even before generating the APK, which is while actually building the application, if a corresponding permission for the task has not been declared, a system exception is thrown by the debugger and the application is forced to close.

So that was all about how permissions work, but how and where do you declare these permissions, and what are some common permissions that are needed while building applications related to computer vision or even otherwise?

 If you already know how to declare permissions, you can skip this part and move on to the next section, which is on commonly used permissions.

Permissions in an application are declared in the `AndroidManifext.xml` file of the Android project using the `<uses-permission>` tag. For example, if the application needs to connect to the Internet, the appropriate permission for it should be written like this:

```
<uses-permission android:name="android.permission.INTERNET"/>
```

The final `AndroidManifest.xml` file should look like this:

```
<manifest xmlns:android="http://schemas.android.com/apk/res/android"
    package="com.example.Application">

    <application android:allowBackup="true" android:label="@string/
app_name"
        android:icon="@mipmap/ic_launcher" android:theme="@style/
AppTheme">

        <activity
            android:name="com.example.Application.MainActivity"
```

```
            android:label="@string/app_name" >
            <intent-filter>
                <action android:name="android.intent.action.MAIN" />
                <category android:name="android.intent.category.
LAUNCHER" />
            </intent-filter>
        </activity>

    </application>
    <uses-permission android:name="android.permission.INTERNET"/>
</manifest>
```

 Note: The permission is added within the `<application>` tag and not inside the `<activity>` tag.

After declaring this, your application will be allowed to use your phone's Internet connection.

 For more information on system and user permissions, refer to `http://developer.android.com/guide/topics/security/permissions.html`.

Let's now move on to some of the common permissions that an Android application may require.

Some common permissions

The following are some of the common permissions that are used while building an application:

- **Permission to use the Internet**: This permission is needed when the application wants to access the Internet or even if it wants to create any network sockets:

```
<uses-permission
  android:name="android.permission.INTERNET"/>
```

- **Read/Write to external storage**: These permissions are needed when the application wants to read from the phone's internal memory or an SD card:

```
<uses-permission
  android:name="android.permission.READ_EXTERNAL_STORAGE"/>
<uses-permission
  android:name="android.permission.WRITE_EXTERNAL_STORAGE"/>
```

- **Accessing the device camera**: This permission is needed when the application wants to access the device camera for taking a picture or a video:

```
<uses-permission android:name="android.permission.CAMERA"/>
```

- **Setting the orientation of the screen**: This permission is needed when the application wants to change the orientation of the screen from landscape to portrait and vice versa:

```
<uses-permission android:name="android.permission.SET_
ORIENTATION"/>
```

- **Reading the logs**: This allows an application to read the low-level system log files. This proves to be helpful when debugging an application:

```
<uses-permission android:name="android.permission.READ_LOGS"/>
```

These were some of the common permissions that are needed. Some other permissions, such as using NFC, Bluetooth, clearing cache files, are also needed depending on the requirement of the application.

Debugging code using Logcat

As mentioned earlier, the act of debugging code forms a major part of the development cycle and there is nothing better than having a tool that makes debugging easier. Logcat is one such tool that helps you put print-like statements in your code to check the variable values or output of certain functions. It is difficult to debug an Android application because it's on your phone and not on your computer.

The Log class in Android helps you print out messages to Logcat. It also provides you with different logging methods, such as verbose, warn, debug, error, and information. The following are the method definitions for logging to Logcat:

```
v(String, String)  (verbose)
d(String, String)  (debug)
i(String, String)  (information)
w(String, String)  (warning)
e(String, String)  (error)
```

An example of how to use the Log class is shown in the following code. This code has been taken from https://developer.android.com/tools/debugging/debugging-studio.html:

```
import android.util.Log;
public class MyActivity extends Activity {
```

```
    private static final String TAG = MyActivity.class.
getSimpleName();
    ...
    @Override
    public void onCreate(Bundle savedInstanceState) {
        if (savedInstanceState != null) {
            Log.d(TAG, "onCreate() Restoring previous state");
            /* restore state */
        } else {
            Log.d(TAG, "onCreate() No saved state available");
            /* initialize app */
        }
    }
}
```

 For more information on Logcat and the Log class, refer to
https://developer.android.com/tools/debugging/
debugging-log.html.

Best practices

A mobile platform is not as powerful as a personal computer and hence requires developers to be extra cautious while building applications for mobile devices. A badly written code can make your application sluggish, hence, it is very important to write the code while keeping in mind the resource constraints of a mobile device, such as limited RAM, limited processing capabilities, and small cache size.

Here are a list of things that can affect an application's performance and should be taken care of while building an application:

- **Memory leaks**: It is important to manage variables in the code properly. Because most of the code is written in Java, the developers need not spend much time on handling memory, as Java does this explicitly. While using C/C++, it becomes extremely important to handle variables in your code.

- **Duplicate data**: While handling large amounts of data in applications that use datasets to train machine learning algorithms, we should avoid having multiple copies of the same data in different forms. For example, if we have an image in the form of a Mat object, and we copy that object to a 2D integer array, then we should make sure to delete the Mat object, as it is no longer needed and uses the space unnecessarily. Doing this not only helps your application, but also other applications that are running in the background. The more free cache space—the more the number of background processes that can run.

- **Network usage**: This is again a very important point. Many applications need to exchange data from a central server or even with other mobile phones using the Internet. It becomes very important to minimize the amount of data that is being exchanged between these devices for two reasons: First, the lesser the amount of data that needs to be transferred, the quicker the transfer time. This will make the app more responsive and the data usage will be lesser (data usage can be very costly at times). Second, it will reduce the amount of battery consumed by your mobile device.

- **Limited computational capacity**: Avoid unnecessary and redundant computations. For example, if your application performs some calculations on an array in multiple iterations and some calculations are repeated across different iterations, try to combine these calculations and store the result in a temporary variable so that it can be used across multiple iterations (without having to compute the result again). An important thing to note here is the trade-off between the computational capacity and memory capacity. It may not be possible to store every calculation that might be reused somewhere in the application again. It depends a lot on how the application is designed.

The preceding list is not exhaustive. There are a lot of other important things that need to be taken care of while building your application, such as handling images (for multimedia applications), transferring data between activities, and distributing work between your mobile and server (cloud infrastructure), which are discussed in the following pages in detail.

Handling images in Android

Have you ever wondered how Android applications are able to load so many images and yet work smoothly? In this section, we will take a look at how we can load images into our applications and process them, without compromising on the performance of the applications.

Loading images

In many applications, we need to load images from the phone's memory; for example, in applications such as Photo Editor or activities with a lot of thumbnails. The problem in doing so is the amount of memory required to load these images into the application. A lot of times even the `ImageView` control is not able to load the image because of memory constraints. Hence, to avoid such issues, it is always better to reduce the size of the picture before loading, and Android APIs provide you with an easy way of doing this.

The following is the code used to compress or reduce the image size before loading it into the application:

```
public static int calculateInSampleSize(
            BitmapFactory.Options options, int reqWidth, int
reqHeight) {
    // Raw height and width of image
    final int height = options.outHeight;
    final int width = options.outWidth;
    int inSampleSize = 1;

    if (height > reqHeight || width > reqWidth) {

        final int halfHeight = height / 2;
        final int halfWidth = width / 2;

        // Calculate the largest inSampleSize value that is a power of
2 and keeps both
        // height and width larger than the requested height and
width.
        while ((halfHeight / inSampleSize) > reqHeight
                && (halfWidth / inSampleSize) > reqWidth) {
            inSampleSize *= 2;
        }
    }

    return inSampleSize;
}
```

Processing images

There are many multimedia applications available on the market that provide users with a variety of options, ranging from changing the brightness of an image, cropping, resizing, and so on. It is very important for such applications to process images efficiently, which means that this should not affect the user experience and the application should not be sluggish. To avoid such issues, Android allows the developers to create multiple threads other than the main UI thread that can be used to do computationally expensive tasks in the background. Doing this does not affect the UI thread of your application and does not make the application look slow.

An easy way of offloading computations on non-UI threads is to use ASyncTasks. The following is an example that illustrates how to work with ASyncTasks. (This code has been taken from http://developer.android.com/training/displaying-bitmaps/process-bitmap.html):

```
class BitmapWorkerTask extends AsyncTask<Integer, Void, Bitmap> {
    private final WeakReference<ImageView> imageViewReference;
    private int data = 0;

    public BitmapWorkerTask(ImageView imageView) {
        // Use a WeakReference to ensure the ImageView can be garbage
collected
        imageViewReference = new WeakReference<ImageView>(imageView);
    }

    // Decode image in background.
    @Override
    protected Bitmap doInBackground(Integer... params) {
        data = params[0];
        return decodeSampledBitmapFromResource(getResources(), data,
100, 100));
    }

    // Once complete, see if ImageView is still around and set bitmap.
    @Override
    protected void onPostExecute(Bitmap bitmap) {
        if (imageViewReference != null && bitmap != null) {
            final ImageView imageView = imageViewReference.get();
            if (imageView != null) {
                imageView.setImageBitmap(bitmap);
            }
        }
    }
}
```

Handling data between multiple activities

In this section, we will take a look at the different ways of sharing data across multiple activities in an efficient manner. There are different ways of achieving this, and each of them have their own pros and cons.

Here are a few ways to exchange data across activities:

- Transferring data via Intent
- Using static fields
- Using a database or a file

Transferring data via Intent

This is one of the most common ways of exchanging information across activities in Android.

A new activity in Android is launched using the `Intent` class. The `Intent` class allows you to send the data as key-value pairs as extras to the activity that is being launched. An example demonstrating this is as follows:

```
public void launchNewActivity () {
    Intent intent = new Intent(this, NewActivity.class);
    intent.putExtra("Message", "Sending a string to New Activity");
    startActivity(intent);
}
```

In the preceding code, `NewActivity` is the name of the new activity that is being launched. The `putExtra` function takes the key and the value as the first and second argument, respectively.

The next step is to retrieve the data in the launched activity. The code for doing this is as follows:

```
Intent intent = getIntent();

String message = intent.getStringExtra("Message");
```

The `getStringExtra` function gets the value that corresponds to the key passed as an argument in the function; in this case, `Message`.

Using static fields

Another easy way of exchanging data between activities in Android is using static fields. The main idea behind using static fields is that they are persistent throughout the life of the program and they do not need any object to reference them.

Here is an example of a class with static fields that can be used for exchanging data:

```
public class StorageClass {
   private static String data;
   public static String getData() {return data;}
   public static String setData(String data) {this.data = data;}
}
```

The `StorageClass` function has a static field data that will store the information that has to be transferred to the new activity.

From the launching activity:

```
StorageClass.setData("Here is a message");
```

In the launched activity:

```
String data = StorageClass.getData();
```

Using a database or a file

This is one of the most complex ways of exchanging data between activities. The idea behind this is to set up a database using SQLite or any other database framework, and use this as a shared resource between activities. This method requires you to write more code. Also, writing and reading from a database can be slower than the other mentioned techniques. However, this technique is better when it comes to sharing large amounts of data and not just simple strings or integers. These are a few techniques that can be used for exchanging data across multiple activities in an efficient manner.

Summary

This chapter summarizes all the possible permissions and errors that a developer can face while building computer vision applications on an Android platform. We also looked at some best practices that can make the applications perform better. In the next chapter, we will try to consolidate everything that we learnt so far and build a simple, yet powerful, application from scratch.

9
Developing a Document Scanning App

In this chapter, we will build a document scanning app similar to Microsoft's Office Lens. This app could cause a huge increase in productivity. For example, you can write down notes on paper and then just click on the image of it, not worrying about aligning it with the device. Then, using some of the algorithms we learned in the earlier chapters, we can detect the page and just grab that portion of the image.

In this chapter, we will directly jump on to the code, and we will see the outputs at every step. To get an idea of what we will achieve at the end of this chapter, let's take a look at the following figure. The following image shows a screenshot of Microsoft's Office Lens in action:

Let's begin

First, we need to set up our Android project just like how we did in the previous chapters. We will use the project ID `com.masteringopencvandroid.chapter9`. We won't be writing any C++ code for this app as this is not a very computationally intensive task that relies a lot on speed. However, if you require, this project can be done using the native C++ code, as we did in the previous chapters.

First, we will declare the required permissions in our `AndroidManifest.xml` file. We will require the camera permission and the permission to save the resulting image to the memory for this project. So, in the manifest tag, add the following lines:

```
<uses-permission
        android:name="android.permission.CAMERA"/>
<uses-permission
        android:name="android.permission.WRITE_EXTERNAL_STORAGE"/>
        <uses-permission
        android:name="android.permission.READ_EXTERNAL_STORAGE"/>
```

Now, we will declare the activities that we have in our project. We need only one activity for the purpose of demonstration. We will call it `LensActivity`. So, we will add the following to our application tag:

```
<activity
    android:name=".LensActivity"
    android:label="@string/title_activity_lens"
    android:theme="@style/AppTheme"   >
    <intent-filter>
        <action android:name="android.intent.action.MAIN" />

        <category android:name="android.intent.category.LAUNCHER" />
    </intent-filter>
</activity>
```

Next, we will set up our layout file. We will call it `activity_lens.xml`. Our layout will have two buttons: one of which can be used to call the camera intent of the Android system and the other one will be used to choose an image from a file. Then, we will process the image that is returned by the system to detect and extract the page from the image. It will also have an `ImageView` tag to display the resulting image, as shown in the following code:

```
<?xml version="1.0" encoding="utf-8"?>
<ScrollView xmlns:android="http://schemas.android.com/apk/res/android"
    android:layout_width="match_parent"
```

```
    android:layout_height="match_parent" >
<LinearLayout android:orientation="vertical"
  android:layout_width="match_parent"
    android:layout_height="wrap_content">

  <ImageView
      android:layout_width="match_parent"
      android:layout_height="0dp"
      android:layout_weight="0.5"
      android:id="@+id/ivImage" />
  <LinearLayout
      android:layout_width="match_parent"
      android:layout_height="wrap_content"
      android:orientation="horizontal">
      <Button
          android:layout_width="match_parent"
          android:layout_height="wrap_content"
          android:layout_weight="0.5"
          android:id="@+id/bClickImage"
          android:text="Click image"/>
      <Button
          android:layout_width="match_parent"
          android:layout_height="wrap_content"
          android:layout_weight="0.5"
          android:id="@+id/bLoadImage"
          android:text="Load image"/>
  </LinearLayout>

</LinearLayout>
</ScrollView>
```

Now that we have our layout ready, we can dive deep into the Java code. In the next section, we will see a step-by-step explanation of the algorithm.

The algorithm

In this section, let's look at the steps we will take to achieve our results. Our first task is to detect the paper from the background. For this, we will apply the k-means algorithm with two cluster centers. With the two cluster centers, we can detect which one of them represents the page and which one corresponds to the background, and create a binary image.

Now, we will use the cluster representing the paper and try to remove some noise and fill in some gaps with morphological opening and closing using a rectangular kernel.

Next, we will try to find the outer boundary of the page and use it to detect the corners. For this, we will detect the contours in the binary image and then identify the contour with the largest area.

Once we have the largest contour, we will detect the lines using a probabilistic Hough transformation. Then, we will join the lines and detect the corners.

Once we have the corners, we will detect which corner corresponds to which other corner, and then apply a perspective transformation to get just the page from the whole image.

The following image shows the steps in the form of a flowchart for a quick reference:

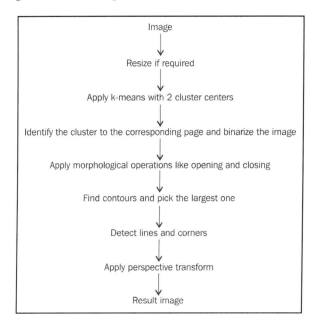

Some of the assumptions and limitations of this process are that the page has to be white in color and must also be easily distinguishable from the background.

Implementing on Android

Open the `LensActivity.java` file. First, we will declare and initialize our `Button` and `ImageView`. Then, will add `onClickListener` to the button. We will call the `ImageCapture` intent, which will open the camera app to click on the image as follows:

```
ivImage = (ImageView)findViewById(R.id.ivImage);
Button bClickImage, bLoadImage;

bClickImage = (Button)findViewById(R.id.bClickImage);
bLoadImage = (Button)findViewById(R.id.bLoadImage);

bClickImage.setOnClickListener(new View.OnClickListener() {
    @Override
    public void onClick(View v) {
        Intent intent = new
        Intent(MediaStore.ACTION_IMAGE_CAPTURE);
        errorMsg = null;
        File imagesFolder = new File(FILE_LOCATION);
        imagesFolder.mkdirs();
        File image = new File(imagesFolder, "image_10.jpg");
        fileUri = Uri.fromFile(image);
        Log.d("LensActivity", "File URI = " + fileUri.toString());
        intent.putExtra(MediaStore.EXTRA_OUTPUT, fileUri);

        // start the image capture Intent
        startActivityForResult(intent, CLICK_PHOTO);
    }
});
bLoadImage.setOnClickListener(new View.OnClickListener() {
    @Override
    public void onClick(View v) {
        Intent intent = new Intent();
        intent.setType("image/*");
        intent.setAction(Intent.ACTION_GET_CONTENT);
        intent.addCategory(Intent.CATEGORY_OPENABLE);
        errorMsg = null;
        startActivityForResult(intent, LOAD_PHOTO);
    }
});
```

Now we will add the part where the result of these intent calls is received, by our activity:

```
@Override
protected void onActivityResult(int requestCode, int
  resultCode, Intent imageReturnedIntent) {
    super.onActivityResult(requestCode, resultCode,
      imageReturnedIntent);

    Log.d("LensActivity", requestCode + " " + CLICK_PHOTO + "
      " + resultCode + " " + RESULT_OK);

    switch(requestCode) {
        case CLICK_PHOTO:
            if(resultCode == RESULT_OK){
                try {
                    Log.d("LensActivity", fileUri.toString());
                    final InputStream imageStream =
                      getContentResolver().
                      openInputStream(fileUri);
                    final Bitmap selectedImage =
                      BitmapFactory.decodeStream(imageStream);
                    srcOrig = new Mat(selectedImage.
                      getHeight(), selectedImage.
                      getWidth(), CvType.CV_8UC4);
                    src = new Mat();
                    Utils.bitmapToMat(selectedImage, srcOrig);

                    scaleFactor = calcScaleFactor(
                      srcOrig.rows(), srcOrig.cols());

                    Imgproc.resize(srcOrig, src, new
                      Size(srcOrig.rows()/scaleFactor,
                      srcOrig.cols()/scaleFactor));
                    getPage();
                } catch (FileNotFoundException e) {
                    e.printStackTrace();
                }
            }
            break;
        case LOAD_PHOTO:
            if(resultCode == RESULT_OK){
                try {
                    InputStream stream = getContentResolver().
                      openInputStream(
```

```
                          imageReturnedIntent.getData());
                       final Bitmap selectedImage =
                         BitmapFactory.decodeStream(stream);
                       stream.close();
                       ivImage.setImageBitmap(selectedImage);
                       srcOrig = new Mat(selectedImage.
                         getHeight(), selectedImage.
                         getWidth(), CvType.CV_8UC4);
                       Imgproc.cvtColor(srcOrig, srcOrig,
                         Imgproc.COLOR_BGR2RGB);
                       Utils.bitmapToMat(selectedImage, srcOrig);
                       scaleFactor = calcScaleFactor(
                         srcOrig.rows(), srcOrig.cols());
                       src = new Mat();
                       Imgproc.resize(srcOrig, src, new
                         Size(srcOrig.rows()/scaleFactor,
                         srcOrig.cols()/scaleFactor));
                       Imgproc.GaussianBlur(src, src,
                         new Size(5,5), 1);
                       getPage();
                  } catch (FileNotFoundException e) {
                       e.printStackTrace();
                  } catch (IOException e) {
                       e.printStackTrace();
                  }
              }
              break;
      }
  }
  private static int calcScaleFactor(int rows, int cols){
      int idealRow, idealCol;
      if(rows<cols){
          idealRow = 240;
          idealCol = 320;
      } else {
          idealCol = 240;
          idealRow = 320;
      }
      int val = Math.min(rows / idealRow, cols / idealCol);
      if(val<=0){
          return 1;
      } else {
          return val;
      }
  }
```

As you can see, we have a function called `getScaleFactor`. Due to the limited memory and processing power of handheld devices, we will reduce our images at a maximum resolution of 240x320. The `getPage` function is where our main algorithm is located. In this function, we have `AsyncTask` to perform our computations, so as to not block our UI thread and thereby preventing Android from crashing.

First of all, we will make our image in the desired form to perform a k-means clustering with two clusters. The intuition behind applying k-means is that the background and foreground will be quite distinct from the background and most of the area will be occupied by the page:

```
Mat samples = new Mat(src.rows() * src.cols(), 3, CvType.CV_32F);
for( int y = 0; y < src.rows(); y++ ) {
    for( int x = 0; x < src.cols(); x++ ) {
        for( int z = 0; z < 3; z++) {
            samples.put(x + y*src.cols(), z, src.get(y,x)[z]);
        }
    }
}
```

Then, we will apply the k-means algorithm as follows:

```
int clusterCount = 2;
Mat labels = new Mat();
int attempts = 5;
Mat centers = new Mat();

Core.kmeans(samples, clusterCount, labels, new
    TermCriteria(TermCriteria.MAX_ITER |
    TermCriteria.EPS, 10000, 0.0001), attempts,
    Core.KMEANS_PP_CENTERS, centers);
```

Now, we have the two cluster centers and the labels for each pixel in the original image. We will use the two cluster centers to detect which one corresponds to the paper. For this, we will find the Euclidian distance between the color of both the centers and the color pure white. The one which is closer to the color pure white will be considered as the foreground:

```
double dstCenter0 = calcWhiteDist(centers.get(0,
    0)[0], centers.get(0, 1)[0], centers.get(0, 2)[0]);
double dstCenter1 = calcWhiteDist(centers.get(1,
    0)[0], centers.get(1, 1)[0], centers.get(1, 2)[0]);
int paperCluster = (dstCenter0 < dstCenter1)?0:1;
```

```
static double calcWhiteDist(double r, double g, double b){
    return Math.sqrt(Math.pow(255 - r, 2) +
      Math.pow(255 - g, 2) + Math.pow(255 - b, 2));
}
```

We need to define two Mat objects that we will use in the next step:

```
Mat srcRes = new Mat( src.size(), src.type() );
Mat srcGray = new Mat();
```

Now, we will perform a segmentation where we will display all the foreground pixels as white and all the background pixels as black:

```
for( int y = 0; y < src.rows(); y++ ) {
    for( int x = 0; x < src.cols(); x++ )
    {
        int cluster_idx = (int)labels.get(x + y*src.cols(),0)[0];
        if(cluster_idx != paperCluster){
            srcRes.put(y,x, 0, 0, 0, 255);
        } else {
            srcRes.put(y,x, 255, 255, 255, 255);
        }
    }
}
```

Now, we will move on to the next step; that is, detecting contours in this image. First, we will apply the Canny edge detector to detect just the edges and then apply a contouring algorithm:

```
Imgproc.cvtColor(src, srcGray, Imgproc.COLOR_BGR2GRAY);
Imgproc.Canny(srcGray, srcGray, 50, 150);
List<MatOfPoint> contours = new ArrayList<MatOfPoint>();
Mat hierarchy = new Mat();

Imgproc.findContours(srcGray, contours, hierarchy,
  Imgproc.RETR_TREE, Imgproc.CHAIN_APPROX_SIMPLE);
```

We now make an assumption that the page occupies the biggest part of the foreground and so it corresponds to the biggest contour we find:

```
int index = 0;
double maxim = Imgproc.contourArea(contours.get(0));

for (int contourIdx = 1; contourIdx < contours.size();
   contourIdx++) {
      double temp;
      temp=Imgproc.contourArea(contours.get(contourIdx));
      if(maxim<temp)
      {
          maxim=temp;
          index=contourIdx;
      }
}
Mat drawing = Mat.zeros(srcRes.size(), CvType.CV_8UC1);
Imgproc.drawContours(drawing, contours, index, new Scalar(255),
   1);
```

Now, we will detect the lines in this image, which contain only the biggest contours. We will try to find the point of intersection of these lines, and use this to detect the corners of the page in the image:

```
Mat lines = new Mat();
Imgproc.HoughLinesP(drawing, lines, 1, Math.PI/180, 70, 30, 10);

ArrayList<Point> corners = new ArrayList<Point>();
for (int i = 0; i < lines.cols(); i++)
{
    for (int j = i+1; j < lines.cols(); j++) {
        double[] line1 = lines.get(0, i);
        double[] line2 = lines.get(0, j);

        Point pt = findIntersection(line1, line2);
        Log.d("com.packtpub.chapter9", pt.x+" "+pt.y);
        if (pt.x >= 0 && pt.y >= 0 && pt.x <=
          drawing.cols() && pt.y <= drawing.rows()){
            if(!exists(corners, pt)){
                corners.add(pt);
            }
        }
    }
}
```

```
    }

    static Point findIntersection(double[] line1, double[] line2) {
        double start_x1 = line1[0], start_y1 = line1[1],
            end_x1 = line1[2], end_y1 = line1[3], start_x2 =
            line2[0], start_y2 = line2[1], end_x2 = line2[2],
            end_y2 = line2[3];
        double denominator = ((start_x1 - end_x1) * (start_y2 -
            end_y2)) - ((start_y1 - end_y1) * (start_x2 - end_x2));

        if (denominator!=0)
        {
            Point pt = new Point();
            pt.x = ((start_x1 * end_y1 - start_y1 * end_x1) *
                (start_x2 - end_x2) - (start_x1 - end_x1) *
                (start_x2 * end_y2 - start_y2 * end_x2)) /
                denominator;
            pt.y = ((start_x1 * end_y1 - start_y1 * end_x1) *
                (start_y2 - end_y2) - (start_y1 - end_y1) *
                (start_x2 * end_y2 - start_y2 * end_x2)) /
                denominator;
            return pt;
        }
        else
            return new Point(-1, -1);
    }
```

The intersection point of the two lines made by joining the points ($x1$, $y1$) and ($x2$, $y2$) (forming the first line), and ($x3$, $y3$) and ($x4$, $y4$) (forming the second line) can be calculated using the following formula:

$$(x, y) = \frac{(x1*y2 - y2*x1)(x3 - x4) - (x1 - x2)(x3*y4 - y3*x4)}{(x1 - x2)(y3 - y4) - (y1 - y2)(x3 - x4)}$$

$$\frac{(x1*y2 - y2*x1)(y3 - y4) - (y1 - y2)(x3*y4 - y3*x4)}{(x1 - x2)(y3 - y4) - (y1 - y2)(x3 - x4)}$$

If the denominator is 0, we can say that the lines are parallel.

Once we have the intersection points, we will try to remove some of the redundant points. For this, we say that the points need to have at least a 10-pixel gap between them for them to be distinct. This number should be modified when modifying the resolution you are working with. To check this, we have added a function called `exists` as shown here:

```
static boolean exists(ArrayList<Point> corners, Point pt){
    for(int i=0; i<corners.size(); i++){
        if(Math.sqrt(Math.pow(corners.get(i).x-pt.x,
          2)+Math.pow(corners.get(i).y-pt.y, 2)) < 10){
            return true;
        }
    }
    return false;
}
```

Now, we will check whether we were able to detect the four corners perfectly. If not, the algorithm returns an error message:

```
if(corners.size() != 4){
    errorMsg =  "Cannot detect perfect corners";
    return null;
}
```

Now that we have detected the four corners, we will try to identify their locations on a quadrilateral. For this, we will compare the location of each corner with the center of the quadrilateral, which we obtain by taking the average of the coordinates of each of the corners:

```
static void sortCorners(ArrayList<Point> corners)
{

    ArrayList<Point> top, bottom;

    top = new ArrayList<Point>();
    bottom = new ArrayList<Point>();

    Point center = new Point();

    for(int i=0; i<corners.size(); i++){
        center.x += corners.get(i).x/corners.size();
        center.y += corners.get(i).y/corners.size();
    }
```

```
    for (int i = 0; i < corners.size(); i++)
    {
        if (corners.get(i).y < center.y)
            top.add(corners.get(i));
        else
            bottom.add(corners.get(i));
    }
    corners.clear();

    if (top.size() == 2 && bottom.size() == 2){
        Point top_left = top.get(0).x > top.get(1).x ?
          top.get(1) : top.get(0);
        Point top_right = top.get(0).x > top.get(1).x ?
          top.get(0) : top.get(1);
        Point bottom_left = bottom.get(0).x > bottom.get(1).x
          ? bottom.get(1) : bottom.get(0);
        Point bottom_right = bottom.get(0).x > bottom.get(1).x
          ? bottom.get(0) : bottom.get(1);

        top_left.x *= scaleFactor;
        top_left.y *= scaleFactor;

        top_right.x *= scaleFactor;
        top_right.y *= scaleFactor;

        bottom_left.x *= scaleFactor;
        bottom_left.y *= scaleFactor;

        bottom_right.x *= scaleFactor;
        bottom_right.y *= scaleFactor;

        corners.add(top_left);
        corners.add(top_right);
        corners.add(bottom_right);
        corners.add(bottom_left);
    }
}
```

Here, we have multiplied the scale factor of the corner values, as those will most likely be the location of the corners in the original image. Now, we just want the page in the resulting image. We need to determine the size of the resulting image. For this, we will use the coordinates of the corners calculated in the earlier step:

```
double top = Math.sqrt(Math.pow(corners.get(0).x -
   corners.get(1).x, 2) + Math.pow(corners.get(0).y -
   corners.get(1).y, 2));

double right = Math.sqrt(Math.pow(corners.get(1).x -
   corners.get(2).x, 2) + Math.pow(corners.get(1).y -
   corners.get(2).y, 2));

double bottom = Math.sqrt(Math.pow(corners.get(2).x -
   corners.get(3).x, 2) + Math.pow(corners.get(2).y -
   corners.get(3).y, 2));

double left = Math.sqrt(Math.pow(corners.get(3).x -
   corners.get(1).x, 2) + Math.pow(corners.get(3).y -
   corners.get(1).y, 2));
Mat quad = Mat.zeros(new Size(Math.max(top, bottom),
   Math.max(left, right)), CvType.CV_8UC3);
```

Now, we need to use a perspective transformation to warp the image in order to occupy the entire image. For this, we need to create reference corners, corresponding to each corner in the `corners` array:

```
ArrayList<Point> result_pts = new ArrayList<Point>();
result_pts.add(new Point(0, 0));
result_pts.add(new Point(quad.cols(), 0));
result_pts.add(new Point(quad.cols(), quad.rows()));
result_pts.add(new Point(0, quad.rows()));
```

Notice how the elements in the corners are in the same order as they are in `result_pts`. This is required so as to perform a proper perspective transformation. Next, we will perform the perspective transformation:

```
Mat cornerPts = Converters.vector_Point2f_to_Mat(corners);
Mat resultPts = Converters.vector_Point2f_to_Mat(result_pts);

Mat transformation = Imgproc.getPerspectiveTransform(cornerPts,
   resultPts);
Imgproc.warpPerspective(srcOrig, quad, transformation,
   quad.size());
```

```
Imgproc.cvtColor(quad, quad, Imgproc.COLOR_BGR2RGBA);
Bitmap bitmap = Bitmap.createBitmap(quad.cols(), quad.rows(),
  Bitmap.Config.ARGB_8888);
Utils.matToBitmap(quad, bitmap);

return bitmap;
```

Now that you have the resulting image with just the page in it, you can perform any more processing that is required by your application.

All we need to do now is to display the resulting image in `ImageView`. In `onPostExecute`, add the following lines:

```
if(bitmap!=null) {
    ivImage.setImageBitmap(bitmap);
} else if (errorMsg != null){
    Toast.makeText(getApplicationContext(),
        errorMsg, Toast.LENGTH_SHORT).show();
}
```

This ends our algorithm to segment out a page of paper from a scene and warp it to form a perfect rectangle. You can see the result of the algorithm on the images, as shown in the following screenshot:

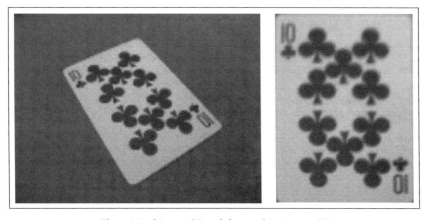

The original image (L) and the resulting image (R)

Summary

In this chapter, we saw how we could use multiple computer vision algorithms to perform a bigger task and implemented a system similar to Microsoft's Office Lens. This algorithm can be extended and made better using better segmentation and corner detection algorithms. Also, once you have the page in the resulting image, you can apply machine learning algorithms to detect the text on the page.

Index

A

adaptive thresholding
  about 20, 21
  adaptive method 20
  block size 20
  C 21
affine transformation 121
Android NDK
  download link 138
  setting up 138, 139
automatic panoramic straightening 134

B

basic 2D transformations
  about 120, 121
  affine 121
  projective 122
  rigid 121
  translation 121
best practices
  about 169
  data, handling between
    multiple activities 172
  images, handling in Android 170
BRIEF
  about 71
  correlation 73
  steered BRIEF 72
  variance 72
**BRISK (Binary Robust Invariant
    Scalable Keypoints)**
  about 74

  in OpenCV 78
  keypoint description 76
  scale-space keypoint detection 74, 75
bundle adjustment 134

C

Canny Edge detection
  about 32, 33
  edge selection, through hysteresis
    thresholding 32
  gradient of image, calculating 32
  image, smoothing 32
  non-maximal supression 32
Canny Edge detector
  about 32
  reference 32
cascade classifiers
  about 83, 84
  Haar cascades 84, 85
  LBP cascades 85, 86
  used, for face detection 86-93
cautions, for building application
  duplicate data 169
  limited computational capacity 170
  memory leaks 169
  network usage 170
Contour detection
  implementation 42, 43
Contours
  about 42
  reference, for hierarchies 44
custom kernels
  creating 15, 16

D

data, handling between multiple activities
about 172
database, using 174
data, transferring via Intent 173
file, using 174
static fields, using 173
Difference of Gaussian (DoG) 29-31, 52
dilation
about 16
applying 17
distance between vectors
defining 151
document scanning app
algorithm 177, 178
developing 175-177
implementing, on Android 179-189

E

Edge detection and Corner detection
about 28
Canny Edge detector 32, 33
Difference of Gaussian (DoG) 29-31
Harris Corner detection 36-38
Sobel operator 34-36
erosion
about 18
applying 18
errors, troubleshooting
about 165
code, debugging with Logcat 168
permission errors 165-167

F

face detection
performing, cascade classifier used 86-93
FAST
about 70
FAST detector 70
orientation, by intensity centroid 71
fast Hessian detector 65
Fast Library for Approximate Nearest
   Neighbors. *See* **FLANN**

Fast Retina Keypoint (FREAK)
about 79
coarse-to-fine descriptor 80
in OpenCV 81
orientation 81
retinal sampling pattern 79
saccadic search 80
feature description 48
feature detection 48
feature matching 47
features 47
Features App
creating 23-28
FLANN 60

G

gain compensation 135
Gaussian blur 12, 13
GaussianBlur function 13
Gaussian kernel
about 12, 13
reference 13
Gaussian pyramid
about 112, 113
creating, in OpenCV 114-120
global motion estimation 122-124

H

Haar cascades 84, 85
Happy Camera project
about 96, 97
faces and smiles, correlating 97
happy images, tagging 97
image, saving 97
smile detector, adding 97
Harris corner detection
about 36
implementing 37, 38
Harris corner detector 36, 53
Hessian matrix 54
Histogram of Oriented Gradients
      (HOG) descriptors
about 93
cells, combining to form blocks 94

classifier, building 94
gradient, computing 93
orientation binning 94
using 94-96
working 93
Hough transformations
about 38
Hough circles 40
Hough circles implementation 41, 42
Hough lines 38-40

I

illumination dependence 57
image matching
about 132
homography estimation,
    RANSAC used 132
verification, using probabilistic
    model 132, 133
image pyramids
about 104, 111
expand operation 112
Gaussian pyramids 112, 113
Laplacian pyramids 114
reduce operation 112
images
effects, applying 2
storing, in OpenCV 4
images, handling in Android
about 170
images, loading 170
images, processing 171
image stitching
about 129
Android NDK, setting up 138, 139
automatic panoramic straightening 134
bundle adjustment 134
C++ code 143-146
feature detection 130, 131
gain compensation 135
image matching 132
implementing 137

Java code, writing 140-142
layout 139
multi-band blending 136
OpenCV, used 137
performing 129
integral images
reference link 85
Intent class 173

K

Kanade-Lucas-Tomasi (KLT) tracker
about 125
implementing 125
implementing, on OpenCV 125-127
keypoint description
about 76
descriptor, building 77
sampling pattern and rotation
    estimation 76, 77
k-nearest neighbors (KNN) 150

L

Laplacian pyramids
about 114
creating, in OpenCV 114-120
Least Square Error 103
linear filters
about 5, 6
adaptive thresholding 20
custom kernels, creating 15, 16
Gaussian blur 12, 13
mean filter 6-11
median blur 14
morphological operations 16
thresholding 19
Local Binary Patterns (LBP) cascades 85, 86
Logcat
reference 169
Log class
reference 169

M

machine learning 149
Mat object 4
matching features
  about 59
  brute-force matcher 60
  FLANN based matcher 60
  objects, detecting 64, 65
  points, matching 60-63
mean filter
  about 6-10
  applying 11
median blur
  about 14
  applying 14
menus in Android
  reference 24
MNIST database
  about 153
  URL 153
morphological operations
  about 16
  dilation 16, 17
  erosion 18
multi-band blending 136

O

object tracking
  about 99
  in videos 99
OCR, using k-nearest neighbors
  about 150
  camera application, building 151, 152
  digits, recognizing 158-160
  training data, handling 153-157
oFAST 70
OpenCV
  about 2
  linear filters 5
  setting up 2, 3
OpenCV4Android SDK
  URL 3

Optical Character Recognition (OCR)
  about 149, 150
  k-nearest neighbors, used 150, 151
  Support Vector Machines (SVMs),
    used 160-162
optical flow
  about 99, 100
  Horn and Schunck method 101
  implementing, on Android 105-110
  Lucas and Kanade method 101-104
Oriented FAST and Rotated BRIEF (ORB)
  about 70
  contributions 70
  in OpenCV 73
  oFAST 70
  rBRIEF 71

P

permission errors
  about 165-167
  common permissions 167, 168
Prewitt operator
  reference 36
projective transformation 122
pseudo-inverse 103

R

rBRIEF 71
rigid transformation 121
rotation dependence 56

S

Scale Invariant Feature Transform (SIFT)
  about 48
  keypoint descriptor 55-57
  keypoint localization 52-54
  orientation assignment 54, 55
  properties 48
  scale-space extrema detection 49-52
  setting up, in OpenCV 57-59
  URL 48
  working 49

Sobel operator
  about 34
  using 34-36
Speeded Up Robust Features (SURF)
  about 65
  in OpenCV 69
  URL 66
Sudoku puzzle project
  digits, recognizing 162-164
  puzzle, detecting in image 44-46
  puzzle, solving 162
Support Vector Machines (SVM) 150, 160
SURF descriptor
  about 67
  based on Haar wavelet responses 68
  orientation assignment 67, 68
SURF detector 65, 66

T

thresholding
  about 19
  constants 19
  reference 20
translation transformation 121

U

U-SURF 67

Thank you for buying
Mastering OpenCV Android
Application Programming

About Packt Publishing

Packt, pronounced 'packed', published its first book, *Mastering phpMyAdmin for Effective MySQL Management*, in April 2004, and subsequently continued to specialize in publishing highly focused books on specific technologies and solutions.

Our books and publications share the experiences of your fellow IT professionals in adapting and customizing today's systems, applications, and frameworks. Our solution-based books give you the knowledge and power to customize the software and technologies you're using to get the job done. Packt books are more specific and less general than the IT books you have seen in the past. Our unique business model allows us to bring you more focused information, giving you more of what you need to know, and less of what you don't.

Packt is a modern yet unique publishing company that focuses on producing quality, cutting-edge books for communities of developers, administrators, and newbies alike. For more information, please visit our website at www.packtpub.com.

About Packt Open Source

In 2010, Packt launched two new brands, Packt Open Source and Packt Enterprise, in order to continue its focus on specialization. This book is part of the Packt Open Source brand, home to books published on software built around open source licenses, and offering information to anybody from advanced developers to budding web designers. The Open Source brand also runs Packt's Open Source Royalty Scheme, by which Packt gives a royalty to each open source project about whose software a book is sold.

Writing for Packt

We welcome all inquiries from people who are interested in authoring. Book proposals should be sent to author@packtpub.com. If your book idea is still at an early stage and you would like to discuss it first before writing a formal book proposal, then please contact us; one of our commissioning editors will get in touch with you.

We're not just looking for published authors; if you have strong technical skills but no writing experience, our experienced editors can help you develop a writing career, or simply get some additional reward for your expertise.

Android Application Programming with OpenCV

ISBN: 978-1-84969-520-6   Paperback: 130 pages

Build Android apps to capture, manipulate, and track objects in 2D and 3D

1. Set up OpenCV and an Android development environment on Windows, Mac, or Linux.

2. Capture and display real-time videos and still images.

3. Manipulate image data using OpenCV and Apache Commons Math.

4. Track objects and render 2D and 3D graphics on top of them.

OpenCV Computer Vision Application Programming Cookbook Second Edition

ISBN: 978-1-78216-148-6   Paperback: 374 pages

Over 50 recipes to help you build computer vision applications in C++ using the OpenCV library

1. Master OpenCV, the open source library of the computer vision community.

2. Master fundamental concepts in computer vision and image processing.

3. Learn the important classes and functions of OpenCV with complete working examples applied on real images.

Please check **www.PacktPub.com** for information on our titles

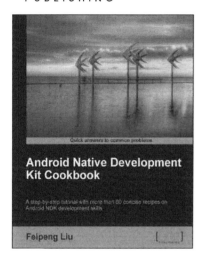

Android Native Development Kit Cookbook

ISBN: 978-1-84969-150-5   Paperback: 346 pages

A step-by-step tutorial with more than 60 concise recipes on Android NDK development skills

1. Build, debug, and profile Android NDK apps.

2. Implement part of Android apps in native C/C++ code.

3. Optimize code performance in assembly with Android NDK.

Learning Image Processing with OpenCV

ISBN: 978-1-78328-765-9   Paperback: 232 pages

Exploit the amazing features of OpenCV to create powerful image processing applications through easy-to-follow examples

1. Learn how to build full-fledged image processing applications using free tools and libraries.

2. Take advantage of cutting-edge image processing functionalities included in OpenCV v3.

3. Understand and optimize various features of OpenCV with the help of easy-to-grasp examples.

Please check **www.PacktPub.com** for information on our titles

Printed in Great Britain
by Amazon